# Dedication

*T*o my husband Don and our children Scott and Heidi, who always showed me tremendous love and support, never failing to keep me on the straight and narrow path when I tended to venture off and try to fix things that perhaps didn't need fixing.

How could I not also dedicate this book to my wonderful grandkids, Sammy, Matthew and Daniel, for being light, funny and never boring, and teaching me what love really is.

# *Praise for*
# Dana's Legacy

Gayle Slate's moving and courageous book, speaks with a clear voice to those of us who care for a child with special needs. The description of her journey is a description of our journey. Her remarkable life is an inspiration for our lives.

*Moisés Barón, Ph.D.*
*Assistant Vice President Student Wellness,*
*University of San Diego*

Gayle Slate has written a book that should be mandatory reading for physicians, therapists, teachers, counselors and professionals of all types who serve the needs of children with disabilities. It tells the story of the heartaches, pain and struggles, as well as the joy and growth of the child's parent who is so often forgotten in the mix. From her experience as a mother and later as a therapist for parents of children with disabilities, she is able to provide insight into the critically important role of the family in maximizing growth and development despite disability. Her daughter's legacy, and Gayle's passion, is promoting the concept of inclusion so that children, both with and without disabilities, and their parents can grow by maximizing their gifts rather than focusing on disabilities.

*Paul Hammer, MD*
*Captain, Medical Corps, USN*
*Director, Naval Center for Combat & Operational Stress Control*
*Parent of a son with cerebral palsy*

—

# Table of Contents

# Preface

*B*eing told I'd given birth to a daughter with cerebral palsy was the worst moment of my life—but also the moment my real life's work began.

Only 20 years old, I struggled over the following decades and did a lot wrong. Gradually, though, I learned to see and accept the wisdom of Helen Keller, no stranger to disability, when she said, "When one door of happiness closes, another opens." And the aim of this book is not just to tell my story but also to point the way for others toward that open door.

My disabled daughter Dana died at age 14½. But, as the title suggests, she left a legacy for thousands of others. After a long period of mourning, I went back to school, became a therapist, and for decades, I counseled parents of children with disabilities, helping many other families not only endure the same trauma but *grow* because of it.

Thus, **DANA'S LEGACY:** *From Heartbreak to Healing* is autobiographical as well as a book of hope for people in pain. It doesn't downplay the hurt, which is real and ongoing. But it offers a hand to the burdened and, I hope, will aid families to gain a measure of control over their lives.

If a child with a disability is part of your life, I trust that as you read this you'll find a number of lessons that will help you in your darkest hours. Among them:

- *Disability brings both tragedy and opportunity.* Although your dreams for your child may seem shattered, new ones can be created.

- *You're not alone.* As not just my story but the experience of many others makes clear, a person of worth and beauty lives within the disabled child's body. Do your best to see it there through your tears.

- *Real control comes when the family faces its feelings honestly.* In truth, how your family responds depends more on its attitude than on the severity of the disability.

- *Listen to your own inner voice.* Trying to make sense out of senseless circumstances is pointless, and dwelling in the past or obsessing about the future just robs you of the present. So to the degree you can, try to step back from the flood of well-meaning advice and listen instead to what your heart tells you.

- *A child's progress can't be isolated from the family's well-being.* You'll likely be dealing with professionals—physicians, nurses, teachers, program directors, physical and occupational therapists, social workers, and psychologists—who have much to offer children with disabilities. But, understand, you have expertise, too. The professionals, by and large, just treat the child, trying to help him or her to talk or walk better or behave in more socially acceptable ways. It's *you* who really knows the family members and their feelings and reaction. Don't underestimate your innate knowledge of what's best for the whole family environment.

# Preface

More important, though, than the lessons I see are the ones you take from this story. I hope Dana's life makes a difference for you, too. I fervently wish her legacy includes a special meaning that enriches your life and that of your family.

Gayle M. Slate
Del Mar, California

*Chapter 1*

# Watching Our Hopes Go Asunder

"Tragedy is like strong acid. It dissolves
away all but the very gold of truth."

*— D.H. Lawrence*

*T*hings began to go wrong around the end of May, 1956, when I was 20 years old and pregnant with my first child. During the last month of my pregnancy, my body began to swell unnaturally. My stomach became very large and distended, shifting all the way over to the left, making my abdomen appear as if it were lopsided. The swelling in my hands and legs hurt all the time. Something was definitely not right.

I tried not to trouble my husband Don too much, though. He'd just started a new, highly demanding business importing clothing from Japan. The combination of giving birth to a new business and a new baby created more than enough stress for any young couple to handle. And though I was worried, my doctor didn't seem concerned. In fact, until the last month of my pregnancy, I'd been healthy and full of energy. The days had whirled by, bursting with excitement about the baby.

1

Then my expectations began to unravel. For starters, my obstetrician—let's call him Dr. Rogers—suffered a serious heart attack just three weeks before my due date. His associate, Dr. Bradford, took over my case. (Throughout the book, I have taken the liberty of renaming some people in order to protect their privacy.) Although Don and I understood Dr. Bradford had an impeccable reputation, our fears began to grow. After all, I had these strange new symptoms, and the new physician didn't know my body or me.

By contrast, I'd felt safe and worry free with Dr. Rogers, my original obstetrician. Because he knew my medical history and how it could adversely affect the birth, he left nothing unchecked. As a result of what may been have mild polio as a child, I'd developed severe scoliosis. At 12, I'd undergone spinal-fusion surgery to correct the curvature, but doctors at that time had only achieved a partial correction. My spine was still badly curved, and the combination of the curve and the spinal fusion could threaten both my life and the life of my unborn child. Because he knew all this, Dr. Rogers also knew a natural birth would be problematic.

## Three times my size

Early X-rays supposedly showed I was carrying a small baby. I didn't believe that for a minute. How could this baby be small? I felt huge and ungainly. The baby was so heavy that I felt constant internal pressure. At only five-feet tall, I weighed but 95 pounds before pregnancy. And already I'd gained 25 pounds and seemed three times my size. Everyone (including me) thought that I looked liked Humpty Dumpty! Just picture this:

five-feet tall, wide maternity top, and a large bow tied around my neck. That was the height of maternity fashion then...and almost laughable now.

Understand, techniques like amniocentesis and ultrasounds hadn't yet been invented. So there was no evidence of anything suspicious, except for how I felt.

Dr. Rogers, after making sure the hospital staff doctors knew everything, had approved a caesarean section for me. He'd also recognized that spinal anesthesia wouldn't be effective due to the fusion of my spine. So the delivery was purposely scheduled two weeks before my due date in order to prevent the baby from dropping into the birth canal. That would also prevent the baby from gaining too much weight and getting too large. As a result of Dr. Rogers' precautions, I'd felt really secure knowing that he was considering all the aspects of my health history for the sake of my safety and the safety of our child.

But now Dr. Rogers' heart attack had changed everything. Even though his associate, Dr. Bradford, had examined me off and on throughout my prenatal care, we barely knew each other. Imagine my shock when I discovered he had different plans for me. After our first appointment, my heart sank when I realized his ideas differed radically from those of my original physician.

## A new reality

Dr. Bradford constructed a whole new scenario for me, one I felt helpless to change. For some reason he believed that I should go through "a test of labor." Earlier plans and the obvious evidence didn't convince him that I couldn't deliver my baby vaginally. What's more, I was too young and unassertive to challenge him. Further, in the 1950s (and even later) doctors were so revered that their decisions were seldom questioned by laypeople. While Dr. Bradford appeared to be intelligent, his contradiction of the plans by my beloved Dr. Rogers threw me into a near-panic.

With my swollen body and shifted stomach, I became extremely stressed by all that was happening and not happening. I couldn't change Dr. Bradford's mind or undo his decisions. So I began to sink into this new reality he'd constructed for me. It was a reality I could scarcely bear but couldn't avert even as signs mounted that events were going from bad to worse.

## An omen

By the ninth month of pregnancy, feeling very heavy and uncomfortable, I was home alone and mindlessly switching television stations when I began to watch with fascination a cerebral-palsy telethon. I'll never forget the young man who walked on stage with a severe gait and spoke indecipherably as he announced the name of the song he was going to perform. He sat down and, with great difficulty, played the piano.

He did so magnificently—but that's not what I focused on. I saw his disability, not the gifts he brought to the stage. I broke into tears while watching him perform, and even afterward I continued to think about how seriously disabled he was. I didn't care about his accomplishments. His performance didn't seem like a miracle to me. Instead, I thought that disability was probably the very worst thing that could happen to anyone.

Stunned, I sat there unable to move, flooded with a fear that just wouldn't go away.

## A powerful fear

At that moment, somewhere deep inside me, I had a powerful sense that I was going to give birth to a child with some kind of disability. It was an omen, which I never disbelieved for a moment.

Isn't it peculiar how things happen? So many times in our lives something occurs—you run into someone or don't, make or miss a deadline, get or lose a job, or catch or miss an airplane or a train—and you wonder: Why did that occur or fail to occur? What if I'd been five minutes earlier or later to that scene? Is there any rhyme or reason to what's happening now? What's the purpose of these events? Are they connected or disconnected, purposeful or random?

Timing is such a huge part of our life, such a noticeable, prevalent, and powerful part of our existence. I'm now sure that seeing that disabled young man on TV didn't happen out of the blue. It sent me a message, and the message shouted: "You have good reason to be so scared."

## One week to delivery

One week before the original scheduled delivery date of June 15 (also Don's birthday), I told Dr. Bradford of my concerns, thinking that maybe the baby should be delivered even before the appointed day. He laughed, reminding me, "Oh no, my dear, I think it wouldn't hurt at all to have you go through a test of labor. I believe it's always better to have a child delivered normally. Besides, your baby has now dropped into the birth canal, and it's too late to deliver the baby by caesarean. You have nothing to worry about. The baby is small enough to go through the birth canal without difficulty. Trust me."

I couldn't believe what he was saying. Chills ran through my swollen body as his words began to sink in. Didn't he understand? The trusted Dr. Rogers had said I was *not* to have the baby drop into the birth canal, I was *not* to have a vaginal birth, and I was indeed going to have a happy, healthy baby.

That was the game plan, the charted course, the expectation. That was the way my life was supposed to be. Even though I more than understood the meaning of each of the words Dr. Bradford spoke, I couldn't believe they would be uttered together in that sequence. I felt as if I were strapped onto a dangerous roller coaster, with no safety mechanism in place, no brakes, and no way out. I felt absolutely no trust in Dr. Bradford, who'd just placed me in this fearful state. I felt utterly, totally helpless.

He made no sense to me. He acted as if he knew my body—and me—better than I knew myself. His confidence began to erode mine. I started to doubt my own feelings. Today, of course, I have strength as a woman and as a patient with rights. But that's not at all what I felt then. Today, faced with the same situation, I'd remove myself immediately from his care, no matter how close I was to my due date.

But being 20 years old, living in the 1950s, and from something of a sheltered background, I didn't even believe I had rights. And I certainly didn't have the strength of will I have today.

Still, I knew then that I had big problems, but I couldn't challenge Dr. Bradford: After all, he was the expert. He ignored me and treated me patronizingly as if I didn't know what I was talking about. In anguish and unable to convince him, I returned home, feeling depleted and almost wobbly. I told Don what had happened, hoping that he would fix it, explain it, or resolve it in some way. He couldn't. In fact, he felt as lost as I.

## Our baby is coming!

Then came the time for our baby to be born. It was a quiet Sunday evening on June 24th, and I was sitting on the bed in our apartment, chatting with Don. All of a sudden, I noticed I was wet and the sheets around me were soaked. I knew right away that my water bag had broken. We looked at each other, realizing this was the moment that we'd been waiting for, although the expected jubilation was tempered by my anxiety and fear about what could be happening inside of me. At first, we both acted nonchalantly, calmly. But then our façade gave way to gave way to nervousness, great excitement, and, of course, great joy.

We wanted to feel happy, so we compartmentalized our anxiety to allow the happiness to unfold. I couldn't contain myself. I was shaking all over with excitement and anticipation. We were going to have our baby! I promptly began to experience mild labor every five minutes or so. In fact, the pains were so mild, I wasn't sure it was labor at all.

We called Dr. Bradford, who told us to go to the hospital. I was grateful for an instant when he said to go. But then made a second statement that brought back the fear and distrust. The doctor said he'd meet us there "when the time was right." What did he mean by that? Why wouldn't he meet us now? Does he again think that I don't know my own body and the messages it was sending? Suddenly, I was worried all over again, and I prayed fruitlessly that Dr. Rogers and all of the countless plans he'd so carefully laid for me would be there now, instead of this man.

## Hopes and dreams

Still, I tried to push away my fears so I could experience what other mothers experience—the joy and excitement of a new human being arriving here at any moment. As we drove to the hospital, Don and I began to talk about our hopes and dreams.

"Of course," Don said, "I'll be happy if it's boy or a girl. In my heart of hearts, I'd kind of like a boy, though. Then a girl. Or, the other way around." He laughed. "What am I saying? Either is fine, and in either order."

"Me, too. We don't have a lot of choice in what we get. But we do have a lot of choice in how we raise him or her. And I want to make sure he or she—especially if it's a girl—has choices maybe I didn't have."

"Like what?"

"Well, like a choice of career. Being encouraged to do great things. And not being automatically ruled out of traditional male arenas, like business. I feel I'm just as smart and capable as my brother, for example. But look who's got the inside track on my family's business."

Don nodded.

"I want our baby—whether a boy or a girl—to become all that he or she's capable of becoming. Not held back by anything except ability," I added.

"Sure," he said. "How could I disagree with that? But what's most important is that he or she experience love…joy…freedom. That's more important than any specific career or tangible goal." He paused, then added with a smile, "Though learning to throw a tight spiral pass is a must."

"No, being able to cook a really good blintz is a higher priority," I laughed.

"An even higher priority than favoring his or her father?"

"In looks or personality?" I asked.

"Both!"

"Now…wait a minute."

So it went as we dreamed and joked our way to the hospital and pondered the creation of our own little family. But hanging over our playful sparring about our future and that of our child's was the fear and anxiety that still clutched me in its fist.

In the 15 minutes it'd taken us get to the hospital, my pains had increased, coming closer and closer together until there was no interval at all between the contractions. Instead, one long, hard, continuous pain wracked my body. And that began to worry me. I'd never heard about labor being one long, continuous pain. (In those days, couples didn't attend birthing classes, so we had no preparation or understanding about the process.) As the pain mounted, my fears returned with a vengeance. I knew Dr. Bradford had achieved his ultimate goal: I was definitely having "a test of labor."

## In the labor room

Don and I were together in the labor room for about two hours, still waiting for the doctor. In those days, mothers first went into a labor room before having the baby in a delivery room. Everything was so sterile and cold. Today, having a baby is much more humane, because moms can have the whole family present during birth in a lovely, welcoming, birthing room that looks a lot like their bedroom.

Having strong, uninterrupted labor pains for two hours was excruciating, exhausting, and terrifying. The nurses were uncommunicative and wouldn't tell us when the doctor would arrive. No such thing as a patient's "bill of rights" existed in those days, and the nurses weren't inclined to reveal much about the doctors.

As the pain became more intense, Don and I were increasingly feeling abandoned. Just when we were feeling totally lost — and wondering if Dr. Bradford would ever come — the nurses began tending to me in a more hurried, anxious fashion. All their movements suddenly became quicker, more urgent, and Don was reluctantly whisked away by the nurses to the father's waiting room. We both knew that something was wrong. I was rushed into the delivery room where doctors and nurses busied themselves with all kinds of preparations, which further alarmed me.

It's hard now to believe how expectant parents were treated then, being separated from each other during the birthing process. Don's absence added to my desperation at such a crucial time.

Finally, Dr. Bradford appeared, seemingly unruffled and calm. I, on the other hand, had now been alone in my anguish, experiencing severe and continuous pain without any letup, for six hours. After examining me, the doctor became dismayed. He frightened me by telling me that I had not dilated at all. Dr. Bradford seemed so surprised because six hours of labor normally should have brought about several centimeters of dilation. Now he realized what I'd known all along—that my baby was struggling to get out, and, as I'd feared, my body wasn't cooperating.

## A terrible urgency

Then the mood drastically changed. A terrible sense of urgency emerged in the faces of the hospital staffers. I was suddenly whisked into an austere operating room where an anesthesiologist was waiting. Before I knew it, they had me sitting on the edge of the operating table, bending over my very large, swollen, and lopsided stomach. The anesthesiologist inserted a large needle into my spine. I didn't know which was worse, the pain in my spine or the pain in my belly. As awful as the injection felt, it wasn't just done once. Three times they tried to insert the needle filled with spinal anesthesia before they figured out that was futile. All the while I was thinking, "Don't any of you doctors know this won't work? Don't you know from reading my health history that spinal anesthesia wouldn't work?"

Still, I was too panicked and scared to accuse anyone. I needed their help desperately. Even if I'd the courage to speak out, I certainly didn't have the energy. I was too afraid an accusation could potentially cause even more pain and suffering for me and my baby.

## In the hands of strangers

The whole experience seemed surreal. It was as if they didn't even see me. I was in the hands of strangers, a doctor who seemingly didn't care and an anesthesiologist who knew next to nothing about me or my condition. It was doubly hurtful to go from a caring physician who'd left explicit instructions for my care, to being treated by Dr. Bradford who willfully ignored those directions and an anesthesiologist who went along with him. They gave me no words of comfort, no words of encouragement. All I saw in their faces was grim determination.

The delivery room became frantic as the doctors shouted directions to each other. Clearly, they were now panicked and working under tense conditions. They had to deliver this baby quickly. Hours and hours had passed since the evening, when my water bag broke, to now, the wee hours of the morning. Finally, they could see that my baby was in distress and that if it stayed any longer inside of me, more damage and possibly death could result. Seeing all this happening while still sitting on the edge of the operating table, I wanted to scream at the green-garbed, masked hospital staffers, "What's going on? Tell me the truth. Now!" But I couldn't scream, and even if I had, no one could or would have told me.

I felt totally deserted. They worked on me as if I were an inanimate object. I remember wanting to freeze time and yell, "Stop! Listen to me!" At that moment, a mask was pressed over my face. And the next thing I knew I was spiraling downward into darkness.

I was out cold. Later, I was told they'd administered gas because the baby's life was seriously threatened. Now knowing that our baby could die, they performed an immediate caesarean. Complications arose, which I'll share with you shortly, but I was advised after the fact that gas is extremely dangerous, even deadly, to a baby in the womb.

## A beautiful girl

"Gayle! Gayle! Wake up!" The nurses were calling out my name and shaking me to try to awaken me. I began to open my eyes, lying very still and feeling heavy. My body was as sore as if I'd been hit by a two-ton truck. They continued to shake me, saying , "Gayle, Gayle, look at your baby!" I slowly turned my head and saw a beautiful little baby, my daughter Dana. Don and I had said if we had a girl, we'd call her Dana, a beautiful name that made us smile every time we said it.

Now there she was, more than eight pounds, not at all the small baby the doctor had predicted. With light reddish-blond hair and big, brown eyes, she was beautiful! Through my tears, I saw that she was crying, too. Though still heavily drugged from the anesthesia, I noticed that Don still wasn't in the room. Where was he? Why wasn't he here?

But before I knew it, the nurses took Dana away—even before I could ever hold her. I fell back into a gas-induced stupor and slept until the next day.

# The awakening

I awoke the next morning, unsure what'd taken place. Had I really been gassed? Did I have an emergency C-section? Did I give birth to a beautiful, healthy baby?

I lie there, excited and relieved that she'd looked so healthy when they'd held her up. I could hardly wait to hold her in my arms.

"Can I see Dana again?" I asked the nurses.

"Perhaps later," they replied.

"Just for a little while. I really didn't get to hold her yesterday."

"We'll see," one of the nurses replied. But she said it flatly, with more of a sense of evasiveness than expectation. And none of the nurses wanted to talk to me about Dana.

I began to get angry, then alarmed. I was having lots of pain after the caesarean. I felt lousy, but that feeling was muted by the worry and panic that began to occupy my heart and mind. I was getting increasingly upset and suspicious, so I decided to walk down to the nursery—dragging my wounded body and the medical attachments with me—to see Dana.

I knew I wasn't supposed to be up and walking alone so soon after surgery. So I sneaked by the nurses without them seeing me. Still, I felt weak. I noticed a wheelchair parked in the corner, so I used it to finish what seemed to be a very long journey. When I finally arrived at the nursery, Dana was not there. Panic-stricken, I thought there must be another nursery with more babies. Then I wheeled to the end of the nursery and saw a baby with tubes attached to it. I felt really terrible for this baby, but didn't know whose infant it was until I saw the name placard on the bassinet, "Baby Slate."

I looked away in disbelief, the shock of seeing her like that overwhelmed me. Then I turned back toward the nursery window, stood up as close to the window as I could, and read the placard again. I almost fainted with the terrible realization that what I'd most feared—that she was hurt or just barely alive— had happened. A nurse then saw me, white-faced and leaning against the nursery window. She put me back in the wheelchair and rushed me back to bed, without saying a word.

The shock was too much. My life seemed to crash down around me, leaving me feeling as if all the blood had been drained from my body. Though the fear very nearly paralyzed me, I asked the nurses to call Dana's pediatrician immediately.

Later that morning, the pediatrician, Dr. Peterson, came in.

"Gayle, your baby, as you realize," he gently began (assuming I knew), "had some difficulty at birth. Then, again, in the middle of the night, the chief pediatrician found her in discomfort and took positive action. All I can tell you now is your baby girl came through both those crises and is doing reasonably well now."

"Reasonably well? What's that mean, exactly?"

He patted my hand. "'Reasonably' just means okay. There's no longer any crisis. She's probably over the worst."

"But when will I see her? What will the effects of this be?"

"In the fullness of time you'll get to see her. There's no rush on that. As for the after effects, we don't know yet. And even if we did, you need to be fully awake for us to discuss them with you. After all, you're probably still pretty sleepy from the anesthesia, aren't you?"

I nodded. But even in my haziness, I sensed he was being purposefully vague. I knew he had more to tell me, and I feared it would be bad news.

An hour later, Dr. Peterson returned and said more. In a professional and objective manner, he explained all the details of what happened following Dana's birth. He said that because she wasn't a small baby, he surmised that she might have been lodged in my birth canal for about three weeks before her due date, and therefore she couldn't be delivered normally. Of course, that's exactly what Dr. Rogers had predicted and meticulously planned for. But, because Dr. Bradford had been adamant that I experience the test of labor, Dana did become wedged in a less-than-adequate space, causing her to suffer anoxia (lack of oxygen). That left her unconscious for four minutes at birth, and she needed to be resuscitated. It was touch and go for her at the very beginning, Dr. Peterson explained.

Then Dana appeared to gain some ground over the next few hours after that initial trauma.

Later that night, the chief pediatrician on his night rounds noticed the fontanel (the soft open area on top of a baby's skull) was hard and swollen. He knew that meant a fluid buildup. So he quickly saved her life by immediately removing the fluid. As the chief pediatrician later explained this to me in my hospital room, he tried to tell me the details as gently as he could: Dana had suffered a major birth trauma.

## How much could a mother bear?

Again, I was in shock. All this had transpired while I was under heavy medication. I almost lost my baby at birth due to poor choices and blatant disregard for previous instructions by my physician. And during the night Dana could have died again had not this nice chief pediatrician saved her life. How much could a mother bear? When I asked how Dana would come out of this, he said he couldn't predict what effect the trauma would have on her life or on her development. He gave me statistics of children going through similar birth traumas, citing different percentages of survival, normalcy and brain damage.

I heard the words, but was too overwhelmed to remember any of them, specifically. Everything was muddled. I felt my heart ripping open. Immediately, the image of the young man with cerebral palsy on the telethon flashed in my memory. The bad omen had materialized.

# Medical experts?

Once again, total strangers, including the hospital's chief pediatrician, were giving me the worst news I'd ever hear: Something was terribly wrong with my baby. I remember in an oddly disconnected way feeling sorry for the doctors and the difficulty they were having in telling me this horrible news. But, of course, my mind leaped immediately to the future as I drew a picture of a grossly disabled adult daughter.

These questions kept haunting me:

- Why did this have to happen to us?

- How was I going to be able to deal with a child with a disability?

- How could I handle a less-than-perfect child when I could hardly handle myself and my reaction to what was happening?"

- Can this really be happening to me?

Marrying so young and going from my father's house to my husband's house never prepared me for this. A deep depression engulfed me. I felt angry, helpless, isolated and devastated. My life, as I knew it, was over.

I kept replaying the events in my mind, hoping that the original scene would be replaced with one where the doctor walked into my room and told me how beautiful and healthy my baby was. I wanted to hold her in my arms and kiss her beautiful little fingers and toes. Above all, I didn't want to be frightened. I wanted most of all to be able to love my baby and see her as all mothers want to see their children, perfect.

I remember saying to the doctors, after they gave me the news about Dana, that I didn't want them to relay this terrible news to anyone else. Growing up, I couldn't bear my parents ever feeling bad about anything. I felt as if I had to take care of them and protect them from bad events or bad news. This was especially the case with my mother.

She would work herself up and worry about everything. Plus, I couldn't bear anyone worrying about me or feeling pity for me. Pity, from anyone, friends or family, was not what I needed right now.

Don hadn't been allowed to see Dana after her birth, so I desperately needed to tell him the terrible news right away, before anyone else found out. We needed to be able to share and experience this together. Not only as Dana's father, but also as my friend and partner, a person I knew I could count on. After the last doctor walked out, I tried to be brave, just as I had done throughout my childhood. I tried to compose myself before calling Don.

Although I was determined not to lose control, the minute I heard Don's voice, I burst into tears. I couldn't say a word. The lump in my throat was stifling me from uttering anything.

"What's wrong, Gayle? Tell me. What's wrong?" Don kept frantically asking.

I could barely get the words out. I stuttered, "S-s-s-something is wrong with our baby." That's all I could say.

Before I knew it, Don was at my bedside holding me tightly. Both of us were crying and feeling lost.

## Sharing a room

The next day the hospital unwittingly and insensitively allowed a new mother to move into my room beside me. This was the first of many awful social experiences that I'd have as a parent of a child with a disability. I quickly realized how different my situation was from hers. The room was crowded most of the day with her happy family and joyous grandparents who huddled and cooed over her new son. My side of the room stayed largely empty and certainly wasn't joyous. Her baby was with her most of the time.

That mother was a nice person, but I was not in the mood to talk, which isn't typical of me. But at this point it was too difficult to make small talk or explain about Dana's difficulties. Every time she nursed her son, I had to leave the room. It was just too painful for me to watch. That was especially painful because Dana was having problems sucking and couldn't be nursed.

My stay in the hospital lasted a week after my Caesarean. Whenever my body would allow me, I would drag myself to the nursery, pain and all, hoping that the scene would be magically different, that Dana would've become "normal" like all the other babies there. Every single day, I prayed and imagined some big improvement in her condition. I hoped against hope that this was all a bad dream from which I'd wake up to find her with all her abilities restored and without any of the tubes that were stuck in her.

But, of course, none of that happened. Dana was placed in a small, austere room next to the nursery where all the other babies were nestled. The "regular" nursery was filled with bright lights and parents, grandparents, other family and friends walking by, cooing at the babies. But Dana lay alone in this adjacent room, with no other baby to make baby sounds alongside her, with no passersby to admire her beauty and see her special gifts.

Dana's room, while separate, didn't appear to have any special equipment to allow her to rest better or feel better. Maybe, I thought, they put her there so that people wouldn't stop and stare at her or make us feel uncomfortable by their comments about her. While the other parents buzzed and around filled the air with joy and happiness, we struggled with our fears, and Dana struggled to live.

As much as my roommate tried to be sympathetic, I knew that I was a real downer for her. She hinted that she felt guilty about celebrating the joy of the birth of her son, while we were going through our agony. Our feelings of loss and our grief increased with every moment that the other mom was in the room with me. I felt so isolated. The other parents created a community in which they all talked about their experiences and expectations: their babies' sleep patterns and nursing habits, about going home with their babies, and their new nurseries.

None of those things seemed to apply to me or to our baby. I couldn't share what I was going through with anyone there. Finally, I gained enough courage to explain to the hospital staffers that perhaps it wasn't a good idea for me to share a room. They then realized that the other mom needed to be with an equally happy new mom. That would allow her to feel less guilty about my situation. And I could find whatever solace I could with my family.

## Chapter 2

# Seeking To Fulfill Our Dreams

"Creating a family in this turbulent world is an act of faith,
a wager that against all odds there will be a future, that
love can last, that the heart can triumph against all
adversities and even against the grinding wheel of time."

— *Dean Koontz*

*T*alk about irony! The day we found out about our pregnancy was the same day Don received his draft papers. We couldn't believe the timing. I remember telling our parents at dinner, "We have good news and bad news. Which do you want to hear first?"

"What kind of choice is that?" they protested.

But it was the same choice as Don and I had—thrilled about the baby, yet anxious and worried about the Army.

I should've known things were going too easily and that our bubble was about to burst. How true that was for me in my early life and for Don and me during the first years of our marriage. When I was young, I would've never believed that I'd become a person of strength as an adult. I was quite overprotected and had little understanding about survival skills. I basically lived in a reactive mode and suffered a lack of self-confidence.

Looking back, it's hard to believe that events could've been so traumatic, so catastrophic. We were married in 1954. I was 18, very young, very innocent, and quite dependent on my parents. Don was 21 and only slightly more independent. We met when I was 15 and became engaged on my 18th birthday.

As our married life unfolded, neither of us was prepared for what was to occur in 1956 when Dana was born, though life had already presented me with some pretty hefty challenges, beginning at age nine. I managed as best I could, but often clumsily. As a young girl with physical challenges, I did a pretty good job of pretending to bravely get through my difficulties.

I was a pretty sickly child. At six weeks' old, I suffered a serious bout of eczema. My mother later told me that I was very ill and covered with an angry oozing rash for months. She agonized over my poor health and tended to me night and day. Being ill became a routine with me. I was more often sick than not until the age of 11. My eczema finally came under control after trial and error with various dosages and medications. Just as this was beginning to stabilize, my uncle, an orthopedic surgeon, noticed that my spine was visibly curved. Doctors later confirmed that I had a severe case of scoliosis.

## Trouble from the start

As I was growing, my spine was curving so badly and so rapidly that the doctors told my parents that corrective surgery was needed. No one knows for sure how or why I developed such a condition, only that it needed attention as soon as possible. Perhaps it originated when I was thrown from a pony when I was five or from a mysterious flu that I'd contracted during the height of the polio epidemic in the 1940s. Some doctors even felt that I might have had a slight case of polio. Realizing that I could become hunchbacked, or have serious medical problems if I didn't have the surgery, my parents nervously agreed to the operation.

To ready me for the surgery, several doctors suggested that physical therapy would help to prepare my body and make it more flexible and responsive. So I underwent intensive physical therapy for three hours a day for almost a year. I'd get up early, exercise, return home at lunchtime, exercise again with a physical therapist, and then exercise one more time in the evening. This was excruciatingly boring for a young girl, but I had no choice if I wanted to get better.

My mother and father found an orthopedic surgeon, an expert on scoliosis, whom I'll refer to as Dr. James. I remember Dr. James well because he was an imposing figure who became very important to me throughout the whole ordeal. He was in his late 50s, a caring, strong, confident and robust man. It wasn't long before I discovered that he was a strong advocate for good nutrition and felt that diet was exceedingly important for healing, especially for his young patients.

As a result, he restricted my diet: no white flour or sugar, which all of my favorite foods contained. Giving those up bothered me more than the prospect of surgery. Nevertheless, I had utmost confidence in him because he made me feel so safe. After Dr. James carefully explained the surgical process to me and my parents, we visited the Children's Orthopedic Hospital in downtown Los Angeles, where, within a week, I found myself admitted as a patient.

# Not a happy camper

Events moved so fast. I had no preparation what was to follow. Before I knew it, I found myself lying down and attached to a rack-like metal table. To me, it looked like a torture device straight out of horror movies. The surgery had been explained to me, but not the steps before surgery. I had no idea that this rack-like apparatus was going to be used to straighten my spine as much as possible before surgery — and then I'd immediately be put in a cast until I was stretched to my maximum height. Although my doctor was standing by me, I was not a happy camper.

They stretched me to 5'7". That surprised me because I was always small as a child. Correcting scoliosis is critical before a child has fully grown. Generally, the entire process takes from one to three years. The doctors explained that although my "normal" height would have been much taller than my present height (five feet), I'd never be able to maintain that height, because the curve would never be fully corrected. Over time, they said, I would begin to shrink, which is exactly what happened.

After the torturous stretching process, I was put into a body cast with a turnbuckle that would gradually bend me into the shape of a "U" to prepare me for spinal surgery. This was designed to bend my spine in the opposite direction of the curve. I ended up having two surgeries within one year. The doctors had to operate through the cast, once my spine had reached its optimally curved position. For an entire year, I remained in a hospital bed in a cast that covered me from my head down to my knees.

## Definitely miserable

I wasn't in pain, but I was definitely miserable. As I say, I wasn't really prepared for this, but what child could be? I hadn't been told that I would be immobilized, a small detail that was left out. Over time, however, I conquered the immobility in very creative ways. Picture this: a child with a cast from head to knees, curved like a U. My arms were free, and I used them! My mother would gasp as she watched me propel my body, cast and all, into different positions, at times swinging like a monkey.

One day, she came in and saw me sitting on the edge of the bed with my feet dangling. "How could that be?" she asked. I was in a cast that would have seemingly prevented me from doing that, or, in fact, from moving at all. But I was determined to have power over my body, not to let this cast conquer me, and so there I was sitting, when doctors presumed that all I could do was to lie flat on my back.

This situation was as trying for my mother as for me. She visited me daily from across town. Still, I was very homesick, which made her visits even more important. She tried to be brave in front of me, but I often heard her crying outside my room. Both my dad and mom were loving, attentive parents, but they tended to be grim. Their facial expressions were serious and intense. To lighten that intensity for me as well as for them, I acquired the habit of making light of things.

My parents did everything possible to make me comfortable and to not feel bad. Even though the doctors told them the prognosis was good and that I would have a "normal" life, Mom and Dad agonized terribly. If they could've traded places with me in that hospital bed, I'm sure they would have. So when they would visit me, they would try to appear upbeat, but it was I who cheered them, which eased their moods and offered them relief.

## The true test

I learned something about myself during that challenging period. I learned that I was not a hothouse flower, but rather a pretty tough survivor. I eventually figured out that I was being rewarded for acting courageously and being strong rather than showing my concerns or fears. It worked better for me to be buoyant instead of crying and feeling sorry for myself (though I often did so privately). My surgeon and I became close friends because he admired my positive attitude. He saw my coping as unusual and courageous for a child of 12. He referred to me as his "champion survivor," which I had difficulty believing but liked hearing nonetheless.

When my parents saw me for the first time in this weird body cast that covered everything but my legs, I thought they would faint. They thought I would fall apart in this situation, but in truth, it was they who fell apart. In that moment, I realized that I couldn't afford not to be a survivor. I had to protect them so they could protect me.

The doctor often brought his other young, unhappy patients in to see me. (I think this was the beginning of my later career as a psychotherapist.) He was sure I could cheer them up. In truth, helping the other kids helped me survive. It drove home the realization that this was a temporary situation for me as well for the others.

After the long hospital stay, I was at home in a hospital bed for almost another year. That's different from how scoliosis is treated today. The surgery is now much less severe in terms of time spent in the hospital and in corrective devices. The young patient seldom misses school and is up and out of the hospital quickly. But in 1947, I was mostly separated from my friends and activities because I wasn't able to physically attend school.

The school provided a tutor, and visits from my friends helped me get through the ordeal. Even so, I felt like an outside observer as I watched my girlfriends move on. I missed out on their maturing process, watching them learn to wear makeup, sharing fun outings together, shopping and flirting with boys, while I remained in my hospital bed in my living room, wearing a very unglamorous hospital gown over my very unflattering body cast. Nonetheless, their visits, my teachers' visits, and my little pet parakeet, (which became my best companion as I trained it to do funny, amazing tricks) all had a very strong and positive impact on my mental state.

Although I had to continue wearing a body cast, at least I was able to return to middle school in the last year and finally participate in school activities with my friends. I was worried that I'd fall behind my friends because of my long absence and feel left out, yet that never happened. Despite the body cast, I was accepted by my peers perhaps because I acted lighthearted and made jokes about my cast. They followed my lead.

Teenagers worry about fitting in, and I was no different, but I was able to carry this off because I saw this as a temporary situation. I'm not sure how I would have felt if the situation were not. I looked forward to a brighter future.

## Free to be me

Finally, the cast was removed. My body was free, and with the advent of high school, I felt pretty normal. Although my spine was far from straight, teenage life brought at last, all the things I hoped for, such as new friendships, dates and fun. My miserable, early youth had passed. My parents breathed a sigh of relief and joyously watched me adjust to my new life. The physical and emotional strains slipped into the background as I became more confident. At last, I'd started to grow up.

Naturally, I was most interested in friends and boys; grades took a second place. My brother Ronnie had a fraternity party at our house when I was 15. I sat at the top of the stairs, peeking with envy down at all the college kids. Don, my brother's best friend, looked up, saw my legs dangling through the railing, and asked who I was. When Ronnie introduced us, I was overwhelmed. I was such a typical little sister, thrilled that Don wanted to meet *me*. He was so cute. Who knew then that he was to be my future husband?

Soon, I developed a crush on Don, but he acted as if he didn't know I existed. As my brother's pal, Don naturally spent loads of time at our house, and I thought he was the most handsome boy

I'd ever known. He was a quiet, nice person with whom I felt comfortable. We were just "friends," and I thought he wouldn't be interested in his fraternity brother's little sister. Then, over time, as we spent more time together, that began to change.

## From platonic to romantic

Our friendship developed from platonic to romantic, even though we were so young. We both had busy and active lives, and yet I felt that Don was different from other boys I'd dated. He was kind and sweet and not caught up with superficial values. I knew that I loved him before he realized his love for me. He couldn't help paying attention to me because I made sure I was around whenever he was at our house. I think he became scared when he sensed that my crush on him was becoming bigger than life. After all, he was only 19 and not ready for a serious romance any more than I was. He made himself scarce, appearing less and less at our house.

When I was a senior in high school, I went to Mexico with a friend on spring vacation, feeling quite miserable and dejected over Don's avoidance of me. Mexico was the perfect get away, and I came back feeling much better about myself and resigned about "losing" Don. However, while I was gone, Don missed me and recognized that he cared for me more than he knew. It wasn't long before we became pinned and then engaged a short time later.

Looking back now, I see that my life before Dana (apart from my recovery from scoliosis) was largely an easy time when our worst problem was wondering when we could get married. Don had a college-deferment draft status and was expected to join the military immediately after he graduated from the University of Southern California. But the Korean War had ended, and the Army was beginning to wind down its draft policies.

We grew impatient with waiting and moved up our wedding plans, thinking that if he were drafted, we could move wherever Don was stationed. In fact, that seemed like an adventure to us. However, after he graduated and still hadn't been drafted, we began to think the Selective Service had forgotten about him. The wait seemed endless! About a year and a half passed—and still no draft notice. We couldn't wait any longer. We thought we'd escaped, so we decided to start our family. I quickly became pregnant, and we were surprised and elated. And that, as I mentioned, was *exactly* when Don got his draft notice.

Then good fortune presented itself: We were spared. We learned from Don's draft board that fathers were going to be exempted. Now we could face the happy prospect of becoming full-fledged parents.

## Building the dream together

During and after college, Don worked for his dad in a men's clothing- manufacturing business in Los Angeles. The company had been very successful until a serious post-war recession hit in the late 1950s. Don and his father, Sam, began to see the business being dragged down by the recession. This was unsettling. Don and I grew up in comfortable surroundings and for the most part never had to worry about finances. We'd been pretty sheltered during our young lives. But with the recession there came, for the first time, real cause for worry about our financial security.

But an old friend of Don's from high school who had been in Japan during the Korean War showed Don some samples of men's shirts made in Japan, thinking Don might be interested in importing them. The timing was just right: Don jumped at the chance to start importing men's clothing from the Orient. And it didn't take long to convince Sam, who was always eager for new opportunities, to join him. Sam had been one of the early pioneers in the men's clothing business and knew a once-in-a-lifetime opportunity when he saw it. Both Don and Sam recognized this as the right set of circumstances for continuing the work they both enjoyed.

Just about the time I was to give birth, Sam was the first to travel to Japan for business, where he'd stay for six weeks. Don's mother, Fritzi, preferred to stay close to home because she was fearful of traveling and had her own interests to occupy her while Sam was away. In the early days of the business, Sam spared Don from doing much traveling because of our pregnancy. Besides, Sam loved to travel and was excited about the direction his business was taking. He was a real pacesetter and enjoyed the challenges before him. Don, being young and a soon-to-be new father, didn't relish traveling and leaving me alone.

Not too many people were importing from Asia after the Korean War, so Sam and Don became pioneers, of a sort, having to deal with different languages and cultures. Their business, naturally, became their primary focus. In fact, it became so important that Sam and Don decided that Don and I would live in Japan when the baby was old enough to accompany us. The prospect of moving there and building the business seemed very exciting to us. But, as events unfolded, that wasn't to be.

*Chapter 3*

# Enduring Days of Misery and Angst

"Pain nourishes courage. You can't be brave if you've
only had wonderful things happen to you."

—*Mary Tyler Moore*

*A*s a young girl with physical challenges, I'd done a pretty
good job of pretending to be brave. But as a young married
woman with a child who was born with disabilities, I could no
longer put on an act of courage. Giving birth to Dana was a life-
altering and frightening experience that would forever affect me
and those around me.

Fears and anguish overtook me, preventing my cheerful
stoicism from resurfacing. As someone who'd earlier struggled
to smile through adversity, I felt that I could never smile again.
Though only two years had passed since the happy time when
we'd gotten married, I felt after Dana's birth as if I'd aged at
least 20 years. Still, I tried earnestly to push away the depressed
feelings and move ahead.

Stress plays a part in all families when babies are born,
even for those who have healthy babies. But that's doubly so

when a baby is born with disabilities. Everyone is affected, from the grandparents down to the other children. The roles in our family became very transparent when Dana arrived. I came to understand that whatever previous underlying problems existed become exacerbated during such a time of crisis.

## Tensions ran high

Tensions ran high in our family. Everyone dealt with the situation in his or her own way. I was consumed with not knowing what the outcome would be for Dana. I felt as if I had to constantly defend her progress to my family. Her slow development caused us all great stress and anxiety, but I continually made excuses for it. As long as I could hold out hope for her improving, I didn't have to face reality. But, of course, this came at a great cost to me.

My family anguished for me because I couldn't face the truth. I was becoming very frail and suffered from continuous colds. I lost weight and had deep, dark circles under my eyes. It was clear to others that I hadn't eaten or slept properly in weeks. I developed colitis, which caused me to experience severe stomach cramps and diarrhea any time I ate a single morsel.

Unlike my experiences as a child in the hospital when I coped with surgery and wore a body cast, this condition did not seem temporary. I couldn't help thinking how bleak the future appeared for Dana and for us, which thoroughly depressed me. How would I be able to physically and emotionally care for her? I could barely eat or participate in life, other than to try to meet her daily needs, and all the while I felt a deep sense of tragedy.

Many say mothering is natural, yet I could not experience this natural mothering and care for Dana because I doubted myself every moment. My worry constantly interfered with my ability to love and care for her freely. I wanted to be playful and spontaneous with her, yet she remained so very fragile.

I worried about breaking her because her body was stiff, rigid, and spastic. The times that I could hug her and hold her were after a bath or when she awakened from a nap, right before her body began to stiffen. I treasured those brief moments when I could hold her in that way and cuddle her as other mothers could with their babies.

My eczema kicked up again from stress, or so the doctor said. Don felt equally helpless and was only mildly distracted by his work. He dreaded coming home to find his depressed wife and ill child, both of whom, I'm sure, caused him great anxiety.

## The walking dead

While Dana demanded all of my time, Don was becoming more swallowed up by the demands of the new importing business. He began to travel more frequently, and when he came home, he was preoccupied and worried about both the business and his little family. He was only 24 and was now responsible for most of the traveling for the business. He had to learn on the job to deal with the ins and outs of how foreign businessmen conducted their work. And he spent an enormous amount of time trying to understand a different language and culture in order to sustain the business abroad.

Those early days presented new and real challenges for all of us; our lives were filled with Dana and her needs as well as the demands of a new company facing international business complexities. Unlike his dad who enjoyed the challenge, Don felt no thrill in working through the multiple dimensions of the business, largely because of what was going on at home with Dana and me. For instance, he disliked waiting in Osaka, Japan, during price negotiations, which took agonizing weeks to complete.

Don could always count on something going wrong on his trips, and that took its toll on him. He constantly worried about succeeding in the uncharted territory that this new business faced. He was over six feet tall and weighed 190 pounds when he began traveling in those early days. But after so much stress, he went down to 154 pounds, due to aggravation and the constant challenges. He always returned home exhausted and depleted. Because of this, he wasn't able to contribute much energy to the care of Dana, and because I was equally depleted at home, I remember thinking that we resembled the walking dead.

In Dana's first year, Don was in Japan a total of six months, spending six consecutive weeks at a time. By then, we realized we'd never live in Japan, despite Sam's urging. Our doctors advised that the Japanese medical community was not as equipped to deal with Dana's medical needs. Even so, Don's father was very disappointed and had difficulty accepting our decision not to go.

## Parents' reactions

Our parents' reactions to Dana differed greatly. In all fairness to Sam, I believe he didn't realize how serious Dana's condition was. He was much more focused on *his* "baby," the business. I think it was too painful for him to admit the truth about our daughter.

We seldom discussed her with him. Frankly, I thought he wasn't all that interested. I know he resented our choice not to go to Japan, but he never directly said anything to us, other than a few sarcastic asides to me. But I never could have gone. I needed to be close to my parents and to the doctors at all times.

My mother-in-law, Fritzi, was devastated about Dana and didn't know what to do. She unwittingly made a comment that hurt me deeply, saying that no one in *their* family had ever had a child with anything wrong with them. This unintentional "accusation" struck me to my core. It touched in me a very deep sense of responsibility because it was my body that was involved in the birthing process. Ironically, all I ever heard from the doctors was the directive *not* to feel guilty. (This, incidentally, has always been standard advice to parents of children with disabilities. But it seems to make parents feel even guiltier, regardless of the cause.)

In my case, although I'd had scoliosis, it was confirmed that Dana's condition stemmed from a doctor's mistaken judgment because he hadn't properly assessed the challenges of natural childbirth on me, a patient with a fused spine. Despite this finding, it was difficult for me not to feel guilty. As life progressed, I began to let go of some of the guilt. However, it was harder for me to shed the anger I felt toward the doctor.

## Dealing with the family

While my in-laws were generally caring people, they felt helpless and didn't know have a clue what to do for us and for Dana. On the other hand, my parents, especially my mom, went overboard to do whatever they could. My parents were terribly upset watching me struggle with my disabled baby. My mother made herself available anytime I needed her, and my dad watched over us like a mother hen.

The way they coped was to do something, *any*thing. They refused to feel helpless. And, fortunately, that was just what I needed then, to be able to rely on my parents, especially because Don was gone so often.

I wished that I could've relied more on my in-laws for support, but, in truth, my mother-in-law was frightened of Dana, something I could understand but found it hard to tolerate. I felt there was only room for one of us to be frightened — and that was me. My mother-in-law was terribly threatened by my parents' take-charge style because it amplified her feeling of helplessness. I tried to be patient with her, but I had little tolerance for anyone who could not be supportive. I was pretty desperate and, I fear, very self-centered.

My mom and dad obviously were grieving for their daughter and realized they couldn't change a thing for me, which was difficult for them to accept. Although my dad investigated all the latest medical treatments and experts in the field, he realized that we were already doing everything that we could to care for Dana.

I also tried all the remedies and alternative kinds of therapies that existed. For instance, my uncle, an orthopedic surgeon, accompanied us to a chiropractor who claimed to cure children with disabilities by giving them mild shock treatments. We went to see him only because we knew my uncle would never allow Dana to undergo anything dangerous. Shock treatments? You can imagine our desperation!

# Enduring Days of Misery and Angst

Like many parents, we would resort to almost anything, as long as it didn't cause Dana to suffer, as long as there was any hope that it would help her. But we nixed "Dr. Shock" after meeting him and listening to his unfounded logic. We continued feverishly down the path of trying to "fix" her. Nothing really worked, though we left no stone unturned.

My mother came to our house as much as she could to relieve me for a little while, whenever I needed her. I was so grateful. I would try to grab a bit of sleep or rest as best I could while Dana would nap. But Dana's medical problems were always there and kept her in such a tense state that she couldn't relax enough to fall asleep. Both my mother and I were often at our wit's ends. My mother tended to get somewhat hysterical, which was not always helpful. She worried as much about me as she did about Dana. Despite my mother's worrying and my father's intrepid personality, I felt fortunate to have my parents' support. Above everyone else, they were the ones I could depend on.

Fritzi never asked to take care of Dana because she felt unable to do so. She felt terribly left out. This often led to problems between the grandmothers. They would sometimes have disagreements because my mother would send my mother-in-law away in a huff when I was trying to rest. Naturally, Fritzi would feel shut out and hurt by my mother's brusqueness, but my mother was more concerned for Dana and me than for Fritzi's feelings.

Some people have an uncanny sense of poor timing. My mother and I both thought that described Fritzi. Dana was an awkward topic, so Fritzi talked about everything else. So when she would visit or speak on the phone, her conversations usually centered on her and her friends, about whom she complained endlessly. Those mundane conversations got on my nerves. I couldn't sit around and listen to her while I constantly worried about Dana. Both Don's sister, Barbara, and Fritzi would feel slighted when they came to visit (without calling first) because I wasn't available. But I didn't have the guts to be brutally honest with them. I only wished that they could've helped me rather than expecting me to provide them with attention, which I had so little to give.

## Torn emotionally

Don felt very torn emotionally, especially when pulled between his dad and me. I recall one day after an extended business trip, Sam insisted that Don come to the office as soon as he returned from Japan. I hadn't seen Don for almost six weeks. Rather than coming home and resting a bit, Don dutifully went directly to the office after a 24-hour flight, so they could talk business. My father-in-law had different priorities than his son did, and Don didn't have the strength to argue with him.

Don felt terribly obligated to his father, who demanded a lot from him. In addition, Don admitted to me, much later, that he had difficulty coming home and seeing me so depressed and helpless. He would've much preferred to go and play golf with his dad on the weekends as a way to rid himself of his tensions. This naturally made me angry at Don because he obviously didn't want to be in our stressful home with me. And, of course, the more I nagged him to stay home, the less he wanted to be there. This put our marriage at risk.

It took quite a while before my anger toward Don began to subside. I came to understand that although I loved Don and Dana, at times I was envious of Don because he had the opportunity to get away for a bit and I didn't. Sometimes I felt, and was honest enough to acknowledge, that I didn't want to be there anymore than Don did. I was in charge of everything having to do with Dana. While Don had an escape route in the form of his business and the "normal" world, I didn't. And I needed a break from the intensity of an unrelentingly monotonous situation.

I noticed that when things were getting too unbearable for me, some event involving Dana would bring Don and me closer. It became a pattern: When her well-being was threatened, we pulled together and grew closer. That was our marital style. Partners forever, neither of us wanted to leave our marriage, and I think that strength of conviction got us through those rough early days. Don was patient and waited for the pressure to abate, but our nerves were so on edge that it was difficult to maintain any calm.

I seldom went out because I feared something happening to Dana. Mom would come and help, or whenever I could have Dana's baby nurse stay, I'd go out to dinner with Don and become renewed. That was a shot in the arm for both of us, even though we knew that the problems would be waiting for us when we returned.

## Isolated and alone

At the pediatrician's office for Dana's first-month checkup, neither Don nor I knew what to expect. We'd hoped that her initial problems would ease over time and that she'd catch up. But what should have been a fairly routine visit was disconcerting to us.

Her sucking and swallowing were delayed as well as her other developmental signs. After the doctor checked her thoroughly, including her reflexes, he tried to comfort us by saying that she was still so young that no one could predict how she would do in the future. "Don't lose hope," he would say each time he saw her, until eventually he finally stopped saying even that.

I didn't need a medical degree to see the challenges that Dana faced on a daily basis. It took so much patience just to feed her. Dana struggled while taking the bottle and was never able to breast feed. Her little face turned red as she coughed and choked at the bottle, making it difficult for her to breathe and making her generally miserable because of her inability to suck or swallow. That's so different from a healthy baby who is calmed and quieted by effortlessly nursing either the breast or the bottle.

I remember very vividly my feelings during that time. It was so frustrating and terrifying not to be able to feed her. One feeding would take hours and even more time to get her to burp. One feeding would often run into the next feeding. I feared that she'd never be able to eat on her own and would have to be tube-fed as a result. Hours of this feeding routine would result in a very hungry, frustrated baby and a mother who felt like an abject failure. When we asked the pediatrician about what to do, he could offer little except for unhelpful advice to spoon-feed her one spoonful at a time and to wait for her to mature a bit.

During this time, we were living in an apartment complex. Soon after Dana was born, I would join other moms and their babies outside in the nearby park to get some fresh air. Immediately, I could see the vast differences between their babies and mine. That depressed me so much that it wasn't long before I stopped meeting with them. It was just too hard for me to carry on conversations and hear about all the "normal" things their babies were doing, while my child struggled to be comfortable in her own body. I was tired of having to explain why she cried so much and why she couldn't raise her head or sit up like their babies. I felt what I perceived to be their pity. They really didn't know what to say. They couldn't comment on how she was developing, so all they could mention was how beautiful she was—and, indeed, she was gorgeous.

But I felt so isolated and alone. I didn't know anyone at that time who was going through what I was going through. There was no one at all to whom I could relate. Everything outside our home was what I perceived to be so "normal" in the sense of being akin to the way that I was raised to think and believe. My childhood experiences didn't involve a lot of interaction with people with disabilities, other than a couple of boys at my high school. They were ostracized by their classmates, and I didn't make a point of getting to know them, either.

I tried to convince myself that Dana would outgrow her problems, but deep down I feared she wouldn't. My fear of something bad happening to Dana prevented me from hiring babysitters. I thought that if I was having difficulty caring for her, no one else could do it, either. If anything happened to her under someone else's watch, I would've never forgiven myself.

For the most part, Dana's eyes didn't shine like other babies. I was never quite sure she was seeing me. She was alternately listless or extremely tense. I'd work hard to make her smile, and when she occasionally did, I was overjoyed. But it didn't seem right for a mother to need to work so hard to coax a smile from her baby. I remember trying all the tricks to get Dana to take a nap, and just as she would fall asleep, the ice-cream truck's bells would summon all the children in the neighborhood, waking Dana up to the sound of the children's squeals of happiness. It was odd that such an ordinarily happy sound would seem so disturbing to me. Then I would struggle to get her to sleep again. Our lives consisted of one continuous struggle, a struggle to get Dana to eat and a struggle to get her to sleep. Everything outside of our house seemed simpler and "normal," yet the exertions at home constantly reminded me of how *not* normal my life was.

## Deficits or gifts?

We made the rounds to all kinds of doctors, hoping to find a cure, or at least to "fix" Dana temporarily. What I came to realize was that the physicians focused primarily on what was wrong with the child and didn't particularly take personal interest in— or even notice—the parents' feelings. We, like so many other parents with children with disabilities, could only see what was wrong with our child, not what was right.

The doctors seemed to address the child in isolated parts—this part needs fixing, and that part is working okay. They checked and tested, poked and prodded, to see what was wrong with the child's legs or arms, or why there was a lack of muscle tone. That was a necessary part of the diagnostic process. But they seldom paid attention to the whole child, her gifts as well as the disability. Rarely would the doctor take time to talk to Dana, to hug her or even to smile at her. Each time I left the doctor's office, I felt harried and hurried along, with thousands of questions left unanswered. Each time I left with my hopes sagging.

Looking back at our case and others, I now see that the doctors didn't seem to have the psychological know-how to deal with the families. Yes, they had medical training, but they hadn't learned how to communicate with parents or even understand how they felt. Parents took to heart whatever advice the doctors gave and worked diligently with their children to help them improve. Some parents experienced a reasonable amount of success, while a greater number simply hoped for a limited future for their child.

When Dana was young, physicians would mostly prescribe physical therapy as a "cure all" for parents to follow religiously without regard to cost or inconvenience. If the parents couldn't afford to pay for the physical therapy—this was in the days before health insurance—they were expected to provide their child with therapy on their own.

## The burden on parents

Physicians always stressed the importance of physical therapy during the first three years of life if the child could be expected to have a reasonable chance of improving. Parents who couldn't afford a professional would spend hours doing physical therapy at home with their child for fear that if they didn't carry out the doctor's orders, their child would fail. This enormous dedication often left the parents feeling exhausted and depleted, especially if the results were disappointing and especially if they weren't doing the therapy correctly.

Those parents took failure personally, leaving them feeling guilty and defeated. Even those parents who could afford to take their children to professional physical therapists felt terribly disappointed if the child only improved minimally. Some parents, who couldn't tolerate the reality of failed therapies, would search high and low to do more, rather than less, for their child. And often their fruitless pursuits left them feeling hopeless and angry with themselves and even with their child.

More doctors are now trying to understand the parents' limitations. With some exceptions, I see that today's doctor tries to consider the family's situation. It's a great help for the parents to know that the doctor is concerned about their welfare. When doctors work in tandem with parents, everyone gains, especially the child. When there's less emphasis on the child's deficits and more on the positive, the way is cleared for the child's talents to emerge. Parents still have to be relatively sophisticated to get what they need for their children. Unfortunately, families with limited or no medical insurance all too often find themselves at the bottom of the heap with no place to go.

## The public's views

As Dana was approaching six months old, she had great difficulty sitting up unassisted. I had to prop her up with pillows in order for her to sit up at a correct angle and be comfortable in her stroller. Everything I did for her required a monumental effort by me. For example, even taking a walk was neither a simple task nor particularly enjoyable. Because she couldn't hold up her head independently, I had to strap her across her chest and shoulders, which put her in a reasonably comfortable position for a while. But she usually couldn't remain in one position for very long.

Whenever I would take her out, I was outfitted like a soldier going into battle. Before backpacks were very popular, I devised my own pack that was filled to the brim with supplies and medications. Only after finally getting our gear ready could we tackle the outing. (Fortunately, manufacturers now take the child's disability and comfort into consideration when designing wheelchairs and other adaptive equipment for kids with special needs. It's still an ordeal but certainly allows the child to go into parks, malls and restaurants more easily.)

Many people typically stop and look in at any cute baby in a stroller. When they would do so and see how Dana was rigged into the stroller, they asked about the whys and wherefores of this peculiar setup. Then they'd attempt to get her to smile at them. When she couldn't, they'd almost always ask, "Is she sleepy?"

I didn't feel like explaining Dana to them each time, so I would nod and simply say, "Yes, she is." I couldn't blame passersby for being interested, but the continual questions exasperated me. I wasn't out for long anyway before Dana would feel uncomfortable and express her discomfort by her piercing screams, causing me to run for cover.

Once when Dana was communicating in this special way, a woman standing in front of me in a line at the bank told me to go home and keep my weird baby out of sight. I couldn't believe what I heard. When I replied, "I beg your pardon?" she repeated it. I can hardly describe my feelings. I was horrified! Instead of putting that woman in her place, I quickly left the bank, feeling devastated. I soon stopped taking Dana out as often to public places. I wouldn't have to face strangers' stares and unkind comments. It was just too heartbreaking.

As luck would have it, I met a new neighbor, Ann, from New York, who'd just moved into our apartment complex. We became instant friends, and she ultimately became my lifesaver. Don and I liked Ann and her husband Lee. They'd come for dinner or bring dinner in to help keep our spirits up. Lighthearted, they made us laugh, and the four of us became special friends.

Many of our old friends tried to help occasionally, but they were upset for us and didn't know what to do or say. So the occasions to be with them became fewer and fewer because it wasn't easy for them to be around us. But Ann would not be thwarted by our sadness. Everyday she would come over and help me with Dana. She had her two little daughters with her all the time, and eventually they became like extended family to us. Ann was a natural mother and seemed unthreatened by Dana's problems. She loved her and was able to calm Dana just by singing to her and holding her. In fact, she had the ability to calm both Dana *and* me, for which I was so grateful. I wished that I could be like Ann and enjoy my baby's gifts rather than worry about the things she didn't have.

## Tremors

Meanwhile, Dana was turning seven months old and was finally beginning to nap and sleep a little better. That was also my chance to rest. I began to feel restored and hopeful that Dana was rounding the corner. One afternoon, I heard some strange sounds—different from her usual scream—coming from her room. They sounded like grunts. When I walked in to see her, she was awake, but thrusting her head and arms forward as she was making the grunting sounds. I was both shocked and scared. I picked her up and held her tightly in my arms for a long time until these strange motions finally subsided. Both she and I were depleted.

This was the first of many seizures, which I remember clearly to this day. I didn't know then what had just happened, or what they were called. No one had ever prepared me for this possibility. I only knew that just as things were beginning to settle down, this new and frightening experience put me right back into my all-too-familiar world filled with over-whelming fear.

During Dana's first six months, we'd taken her to pediatricians who were standouts in their field. I also began during this time to read everything I could about children with disabilities. (However, not a lot had been written outside of the medical community.) Once again, the image returned: I couldn't forget the young man from the United Cerebral Palsy telethon that I'd watched when I was pregnant. I felt as if my worst fears were coming true.

I connected Dana's symptoms with my readings and became convinced that she had cerebral palsy, a disorder caused when a severe lack of oxygen to the brain affects motor development. Depending on the amount of brain damage, the severity of the child's condition can vary from mild to severe. This would have been a direct result of what happened during Dana's birth. So when the diagnosis of cerebral palsy finally came, I was dispirited but not surprised.

By this time I'd changed pediatricians, going from one who knew little about disabilities to another who was an expert on cerebral palsy. In fact, he sat on the board of the local United

Cerebral Palsy Foundation. He came highly recommended, and his qualifications reassured me that this time I could count on this doctor to be in our corner. When I called to talk to him about the seizure, I learned that he was away. I tried not to feel too anxious and told myself that the seizure was probably a one-time event and not to worry. However, the next day the same thing happened at exactly the same time, right after her nap.

This time the seizure was more violent and lasted longer. Without hesitation, I frantically called my pediatrician's associate (lucky me, another associate!) and spoke to him hysterically. To this day, I can't believe what he replied: "Give her an aspirin, and she will calm down."

Why would she need an aspirin? Can a seizure be controlled with aspirin? What's more, how could she take an aspirin when she can't even swallow?

I panicked! I couldn't believe that once again, a physician was failing me and my daughter. I called my friend Ann, who immediately drove us to the doctor's. I stormed unannounced into his office, bypassed his receptionist, and placed my seizing daughter on top of his desk, right in front of him, and in exasperation, yelled, "*You* give her an aspirin!"

That frustrating experience and many more seizures led us to seek opinions from several pediatric neurologists, all of whom agreed, after assessing her electro-encephalograms, that Dana was epileptic and needed to be on medication for probably the rest of her life. (Electroencephalograms are used to detect brain damage and seizure activity.) Once again Don and I were struck down by the terrible diagnosis and, even worse, the prognosis.

## *Deep frustrations*

Months passed as the doctors tried to regulate the seizures using different medications. They finally settled on Dilantin, which had many side effects, but it was the drug most effective for Dana. In the 1950s, the choices of medications were limited. Eventually, the seizures disappeared, but they'd had an impact on Dana. She regressed even more as a result of the seizures. She was prone to catching colds, which also destroyed whatever little progress she'd made. The Dilantin also was beginning to rot her teeth, but we couldn't find another medication that was as effective in controlling the seizures. We learned that children with these kinds of challenges typically make progress, then regress or stay on a plateau for months. We were deeply frustrated.

Just when we felt like giving up, Dana would make some real strides. I lived for these occasions. Even though Dana couldn't move freely, she would sometimes look up at me and smile. That was all that I needed to keep going. I'd work so hard to get Dana to respond to me, and when she would, I'd be elated. We put great effort into stimulating her with toys, singing, and all kinds of attention-getting behaviors. It was exhausting. When a child can't give immediate feedback to his or her parents, it's so disheartening. I'd never before realized how much a child's smile mattered.

As a result of feeling disheartened, I became further isolated. I avoided being with people, now out of fear that Dana would become ill. Because she was very susceptible, I kept her in a figurative bubble. I couldn't bear to have her lose ground over and over again. I also couldn't help identifying with Dana and feel disabled myself.

## Chapter 4
# Facing a Turning Point

"Some men have thousands of reasons why
they cannot do what they want to, when all they need
is one reason why they can."

—*Willis Whitney*

*O*ur new pediatrician, Dr. Glass, helped by providing new information about resources for Dana, specifically an early-intervention program at UCLA. The program was directed by developmental pediatrician Dr. Janss, a renowned specialist on cerebral palsy (CP). "If anyone could help Dana," Dr. Glass said, "Dr. Janss is the person."

UCLA was the only place I knew of during the 1950s that provided early intervention for babies and children with disabilities. Meeting Dr. Janss was both exciting and anxiety-producing for Don and me. We eagerly went to meet this petite, wrinkled, elderly woman who wore a crisp white coat and specs halfway down her nose. Her graying hair was pulled into a topknot. She was pleasant but business-like.

We'd been told that she was the foremost CP expert and had dedicated her life to aiding children with disabilities. In fact, she spent much of her time consulting and speaking to national groups. What free time she had she spent largely in the outdoors, mostly hiking, but her primary avocation was helping her patients. (I reconnected by phone with Dr. Janss and learned that she'd married for the first time at age 85. Unfortunately, her wedded bliss lasted only four years when her beloved husband died. In fact, she was interviewed in a book about famous women in which she talked openly about her sex life with her new husband. She shared that she couldn't believe that she'd lived 85 years without experiencing sexual intimacy. She felt so fortunate to discover this before she died. This was not the stodgy pediatrician I knew, now so forthright and expressive. It goes to show that you're never too old for new life experiences. She died at the age of 93.)

Dr. Janss was soft-spoken, but very direct with us. After asking us many questions, she turned her attention to Dana, giving her the most extensive examination yet. The doctor was extremely serious in her approach, but Dana didn't seem to mind. Dr. Janss's gentle probing and reflex testing seemed to calm Dana (unlike what happened in previous medical exams.) We were heartened when Dr. Janss confirmed that Dana would be accepted into her program.

The not-so-good news was that Dr. Janss didn't really know how much progress Dana could make because the brain damage was significant. She emphasized that if Dana was to improve, she had to be involved for the next few years in intensive physical and occupational therapy along with lots of stimulation that would be provided as part of the program. The doctor told us that progress tends to slow after initial improvements. She also gave us heartbreaking news that children with such serious developmental delays tend to live shorter lives, often dying around the age of puberty.

At this point, we couldn't believe that Dana, because she was still so young, would be so profoundly delayed. Nor were we willing to accept that she could be taken from us at such a young age. Our dream for a healthy child continued to elude us. Despite that, we kept hoping.

## The UCLA program

We immediately signed Dana up for the UCLA program, which would last two years. There we met other parents with whom we became really close friends. It was also there that I could talk for the first time to other parents who understood what we were going through.

The children in the program had varying diagnoses: some mild, some more severe. Some had Down Syndrome, some had developmental delays, and most had CP. I don't remember any child with Autism. Although Dana had finally been officially diagnosed with CP, it was way too early to really know the severity of her condition. In any case, I couldn't have accepted a serious diagnosis at that time.

I became more acquainted with the mothers who brought their children twice a week to the program. We would sit behind a one-way mirror in a small, darkened room and observe the various therapists, volunteers and teachers who worked and played with our children. We also had ample time to carefully watch our children while we were talking to each other. One source of hidden guilt for me was that I couldn't stop comparing Dana to the other kids, who were progressing. I later discovered from our conversations that I wasn't the only one making comparisons. This was pretty typical for many of the parents. It felt good to finally be open with other parents and find that they, too, occasionally felt the same way.

Mostly toddlers attended the program, with few exceptions. The room was large and airy and resembled a regular preschool setting, except for the therapeutic equipment for the children. All kinds of orthopedic contraptions existed to help the children sit, stand and walk. As in most preschools, music, art and slides and swings were available for the children who were able to use them. Regardless of the limitations of his or her disabilities, every child got stimulation in this generally bright, happy environment.

The children loved to sit in the train that the therapists pulled outside to take them to play. From time to time we were called in to confer with and work alongside the professionals, who included occupational, physical, speech, and language therapists. But for the most part, we remained behind the one-way mirror observing and talking to each other about our kids.

Although we appreciated all the input our children were receiving, one couldn't help feeling as though the professionals were the authorities and the parents were the recruits. I always desired more of a partnership in this process, but I said little at that time. I comforted myself with the thought that, at the very least, Dana was finally getting real help. We felt encouraged, and our hopes were definitely up.

# A new support system

Don and I became close friends with Margie and Hal, who had a son named Mark, in the program. In addition, we were friendly with several other couples there. In fact, our social lives became increasingly centered on people who had children with disabilities. We'd have barbecues and parties together. Although our close friends outside this circle were still standing by us, we felt less constrained being with other parents of kids with special needs.

This freed us from needing to constantly explain to others what was going on in our lives. We had so little energy or interest left over to socialize. How could others understand how we felt? It was always difficult to be in social situations, such as celebrating our friends' children's birthdays We felt the sting of reality when we watched children the same age as Dana run and play. I put on an act as if everything was okay, but in truth, I was experiencing loss each time we were together.

So our conversations with the parents of children with disabilities seemed more relevant. We could cut right to the core, without worrying about carefully selecting words that might offend or turn off those in different circumstances. We knew that while most parents couldn't possibly understand what we were going through, we shared much common ground with parents who had children with disabilities.

This common ground later inspired me to work with children with disabilities and to create groups for their parents. Even with the closeness between the parents, real differences existed within our social group between the fathers and mothers so far as their ability to discuss their child's problems freely. Talk among the mothers almost always centered on doctors, different ways to cope with the children's situations, and always on what was going wrong.

The dads generally had an equally hard time accepting their children's disability and tended to talk in the group more about sports or other matters unrelated to the child. You could feel their level of discomfort by their avoidance. Eventually, many of the dads began to feel more comfortable in facing their own disappointments and learned to bond with the other dads going through similar experiences. Once that occurred, conversations among all the parents became more honest. The moms and dads, finally, were able to talk more easily and directly to each other both in and out of the group.

We spoke more readily about the effect our children had on our lives, feelings, and relationships. Occasionally, the wives complained about their husbands' general lack of involvement and unwillingness to take more responsibility in parenting. The dads, in turn, complained that they often felt relegated to a secondary position in their family and felt they couldn't do as good a job as their wives, which caused hard feelings between the couple. It's true that the moms often were too nervous to let go of the sense of control they experienced by feeling that no one else could do the job as well as they. Amazingly, after the moms confessed this in the group, they began to relinquish more control to their husbands.

There were exceptions, of course. Some fathers were willing and delighted to take on the job of actively raising their child and talked openly about their feelings. They just weren't the majority. Like me, many parents seemed to isolate themselves from the outside world, which seemed disinterested and unsupportive. Like many others who experience traumatic times, parents of children with disabilities often feel their broken hearts and sadness prevent them from connecting with almost anyone outside their situation. It's almost as if they automatically expect others to understand what they're going through, even when they don't communicate or ask for help.

It makes parents feel vulnerable to ask for assistance. If outsiders can't readily understand, we parents almost feel resentful toward them for creating a no-win situation for everyone. I was fortunate to at least find some special people, like my cousin Marilyn and my friend Ann, who were more than willing and available to listen and lend a helping hand.

## Struggling to survive

Margie and Hal had a teenage daughter, Leslie, in addition to their son Mark. Margie was a good mother to both children, but like many mothers of children with disabilities, she spent an inordinate amount of time with her son whose CP made him completely dependent on her. In many ways he was similar to Dana, having severe disabilities.

For a long while, we really had a great time with Hal and Margie. It was comforting to be able to have another warm couple in our lives. We didn't have to explain anything to them. They just knew. At times, however, dark clouds hovered. Margie appeared calm and unflappable; Hal was the intense one in the relationship. As our friendship grew, we began to be aware of problems arising in their marriage.

Noticeable tension between Margie and Hal began to develop. Marge had less and less time for her husband, which he began to resent. She spent most of her time meeting her son's needs while also dealing with her daughter's periodic resentment and clamor for attention. Her husband was a hard-working businessman who traveled often to Japan, much like Don. Margie fared better than I during those absences.

Meanwhile, Don and Hal built their relationship on their commonalities and became good friends. By this time, sadly, our dear friends Ann and Lee moved away. Consequently, our friendship with them became a long-distance relationship. I've always felt so grateful to have had them in our lives. But their move allowed us to become even closer to Margie and Hal, which also meant we saw more and more of the tension growing between them.

Although Hal cared deeply for his children and was involved with them, he needed his wife even more. She either could not or chose not to live up to his demands for her attention. His criticism of her would lead to standoffs between them. Hal felt that Mark did not need as much time as Margie gave him, while Margie felt that no one else could care for Mark as well as she could. That seemed more apparent as Mark grew older. Hal resorted to traveling to Japan more often. They became more and more distant from each other, which eventually led to their divorce a few years later.

# Family tension

Having a child who's ill or has disabilities is bound to create family tension and underscore problems that might otherwise be easily resolved. In fact, the divorce rate for families with children with disabilities hovers around 75 percent and seems to be increasing each year. Parents know this and try their hardest not to become a statistic, but the pressure plays havoc with the relationship.

The differences between them directly affect their adjustment, their acceptance of themselves, and their situation. All this can become too much for some marriages to endure. It becomes difficult for these parents to maintain balance in their lives when there's no outside support. With all the constant challenges they face, maintaining balance can occur if they miraculously adapt to their situation. Naturally, as a family therapist, I feel the best way to afford them the opportunity to be honest and forthright with their partner is by going to therapy with a trusted counselor. Going sooner rather than later gives them a better chance to beat the odds.

Parents need to believe that they're deserving of better lives. Too many parents blame themselves and each other for their child's disability, preventing any chance for their marriage to succeed. How can they feel differently if they have no one to talk to and no one to help them cope more effectively?

## Different styles

Although Don and I had many difficulties, somehow we were able to overcome them over time. Although Don protested that he was too busy to go into counseling, I went alone to a psychotherapist and found out much about the two of us. I had to learn to back off and allow Don more space. I only figured out much later that nagging and begging wasn't going to help any of us, Dana included. I knew that we both were persevering in terms of wanting to stay together. We always deeply valued the sanctity of our marriage and wanted to be together for the long haul. Interestingly, Don today is a loyal proponent of therapy, having experienced life and its difficulties. He just got to this place a little later than me.

Our family backgrounds and values differed from that of Margie and Hal. Hal had generally unhappy family relationships and looked to Margie for attention and approval. Enmity existed between Hal and his siblings, and divorce was common in his family. Margie, on the other hand, felt more secure within her family, although her dad died when she was young. She was always being helped by her supportive mother, who lived with them, and by her sister who lived close by.

Hal was generous to his mother-in-law and appreciated the care she showed her daughter and grandchildren. But he would have preferred that Margie allow her mother to take care of Mark more often so Marge and Hal could be together. When they did go out, Margie usually couldn't wait to return home to be with Mark. This made Hal feel resentful and unimportant, giving him the impression Margie preferred Mark's company to his.

Don's family and my family, although far from perfect, were intact and shared generally good feelings toward each other. I think the difference between Don and Hal was that Don's needs were different than Hal's. Don had always demonstrated an independence and rarely put demands on people. Though he wasn't as needy for my attention as I was for his, little doubt existed in my mind that Don cared about me and about our marriage. Nevertheless, he did retreat to his comfort level, which meant being involved in his business more than with Dana.

When it came to Dana, I knew he had real fears about knowing how to be a father to her and handling her. How much I wished he could be her father in every sense of the word, but he could not relate to her, mostly because she did not relate to us. I needed Don in the same way that Hal needed Margie, for affection, support and someone to talk to. Margie, unlike me, didn't seem to need Hal for these things. She was more even-tempered than I, and most of the time she felt she could handle everything on her own. She felt more at ease in her parenting skills and suffered less anguish than I. That stemmed partly, I think, from the fact that Mark was her second child. Perhaps Don and I might have been different if Dana hadn't been our first child.

Don and I had different styles of communication. When I was sad or depressed during the most difficult periods of Dana's life, I would say, "Don, why don't you come home a little earlier tonight?"

"I'm awfully busy right now," he'd reply. "But I'll try if I can."

But, in truth, he seldom came home early. When he did, I'd sometimes press him at night to talk to me about anything, but usually about Dana. He'd usually respond with silence or read. I'd press him.

"Don, talk to me. Tell me your thoughts. Do you see any progress by Dana? If so, what? Can't you see that I'm starved for observations other than my own?"

"What do you want me to say?" he'd answer.

Actually, we were both stressed and terribly upset, and he would shut down if he felt threatened by my pleas for his attention. After spending all day with Dana, I clamored for Don's attention.

Our different styles made me unhappy. He had to get away to forget the problems, and I couldn't think about anything else but the problems and a search for solutions. Neither of us was sure where we were headed.

Our marriage suffered, but because of therapy, we made it through. I figured out that Don would be responsive if I left him alone for a while. If I had an urgent problem that centered on Dana rather than on us, he could come through and be more responsive to me. It was just hard for Don to know when I wasn't anxious or feeling desperate because that was my prevailing mood.

## Little progress

Meanwhile, as Dana grew, she made little progress. By the time she turned two, I could see that she was seriously developmentally delayed. I was extremely worried about her future. After she graduated from the UCLA program where I felt she was safe and happy, we didn't know where she would continue. At that time in the late 1950s and early '60s, there was absolutely no place for her to go. As the time was approaching for her to leave UCLA, I became plagued with constant sore throats and continuous colds. As I became more anxious about coming to the end of the line, I knew these fears were making me ill.

Margie and Hal were equally worried. Mark, a year older than Dana, showed only a little more improvement than Dana. He clearly responded to those around him, unlike Dana. Yet he still required education, physical therapy and constant stimulation, which was not automatically available as it is today.

We visited the few places that were recommended and available to the kids after leaving UCLA, but they proved to be awful. Nothing more than colorless holding tanks for kids with disabilities, they offered little therapy and even fewer opportunities for stimulation. They also weren't age-appropriate for our children—young adults were mixed with young children with every kind of disability imaginable. It was as if all the children with all kinds of disabilities were thrown together without any thought of ever helping them, only of warehousing them. It was worse than any horror movie I'd ever seen. No one had a real chance to improve under those circumstances.

Meanwhile, without our knowledge, my father had been contacting various physicians to explore the possibility of placement for Dana. I suspect that my dad wasn't able to tolerate seeing me so upset and physically ill because of my constant worry about Dana. He felt my anguish and pain and acted on this without seeking our permission. It was obvious that he was suffering more for us than for his granddaughter.

When I discovered this, I was annoyed with him because of his interference, but I also understood that he was trying to control the situation as he usually did in our family. This was pretty typical of my dad. He was terribly concerned when any of us had problems. He felt that he had to do something to help us and thought he had the power to change things to make life easier and better for his family.

## Placement pondered

I was concerned that this time he could be right and the result would be a serious choice for us. He arranged a visit with a particular neurologist and urged us to see him. Don and I saw him mainly to talk about Dana's condition. In truth, I believe my father had arranged for this physician to convince us to place Dana. When this physician told us, after a cursory examination, that Dana would never improve, we were upset. He advised us to consider placement for her. He actually recommended that we place her as far away as we could and then never see her again. We were aghast! He went too far. He hardly knew Dana, and he certainly didn't know us at all.

Placement wasn't something I was ready to consider. After all, this was our baby. Although I refused to talk about placement, I couldn't stop thinking about it. Don, of course, went along with me, but probably felt some relief in confronting the subject. We shared this with Margie and Hal, who were upset for us. But after much agonizing with Margie and taking into account the poor quality of the available schools, she and I, along with our husbands, decided to entertain the idea and look at the various placement facilities in or near Los Angeles, where we lived. I was hoping that I wouldn't have to place Dana. But somewhere inside me, I knew I had to learn what was available.

## Facing reality

Realizing my limitations in caring for Dana, I finally faced reality when I turned 23. I then understood that I wasn't equipped emotionally or physically to care for her, to meet her needs in a manner that would allow her to have the quality of life that I so desperately wanted for her.

I knew that she would always have severe disabilities and that maybe no one else could provide her with a quality life, either. But I didn't come to that conclusion quickly or painlessly. There was no place for her to go after the UCLA program. There was no way out for her *or* for me. I could no longer fool myself. As I write these words, I can see clearly how much this was more about me than about Dana. My feelings of being overwhelmed swallowed me whole. After Dana had been born, I came to believe that having other children wouldn't be possible. Because Dana required so much of me, I wouldn't have energy to care for another child. And I thought that I loved Dana so much that I couldn't possibly love another child enough.

Meanwhile, Margie was beginning to see that her marriage was in jeopardy. Feeling ambivalent, she also began to consider placement for Mark, provided that it was quality care. However she too, was battling the guilt of abandoning her child.

I couldn't stand the thought of giving Dana up to be in someone else's care. I knew that I resisted placement so strongly because I couldn't bear feeling like a failure as a mother. The guilt would be too overwhelming. After all, the only thing I ever wanted to be was a mother, a really good mother.

*Chapter 5*

# Confronting the
# Second Death

"Life is easier than you think; all that is necessary
is to accept the impossible, do without the
indispensable and bear the intolerable."

*— Kathleen Norris*

$\mathcal{M}$argie, though concerned about placing her son, didn't have her heart in pressing on with the search. So I began to make the rounds myself and give her feedback on what I'd found. I visited a few places that held no appeal whatsoever for me. In fact, it was very depressing to see people put away for life in these places.

I suppose there was nothing really wrong with these institutions. They were clean, and the caretakers were nice enough. But places were sterile, without joy or life. They felt like a dead end to me, and I couldn't imagine Dana in a place like this surrounded by other children with disabilities. I didn't want to see my Dana that way because I didn't think of her as being as disabled as these others. (Who was I kidding?) There was little friendly chatter with the children. In fact, no one really talked to them much. The children were cleanly dressed, given food, and generally left alone. Nothing seemed to exist inside or outside the walls for these children.

The California state institution was worse, I initially thought, because it used older people with disabilities as aides to help with the youngsters. I was stunned, thinking these people couldn't possibly know enough to share their love, or have the ability to understand or meet the children's needs. Then, I saw that the caretakers with disabilities were trained well enough to care for the littler ones and in fact, were warmer and sweeter to the children than in the previous place I'd visited, where the caretakers were able-bodied and efficient but distant.

## A different light

This is when I began to see people with disabilities in a different light. I began to realize they were as human and blessed with the ability to love as anyone else, perhaps even more so. I began to connect with their warmth and openness. Their eagerness to help and to please remained unspoiled by the ravages of ordinary life. Although I could never place Dana in a state institution, the idea of placement was becoming more acceptable to me as long as the place was clean, attractive, and staffed with people who were loving toward the children.

The more I resisted the notion that Dana's disabilities would never be as severe as those of the kids in the state facility, the more I came to realize I was fooling myself, and that it might be just a matter of time before Dana would need to be placed somewhere. I knew deep down in my heart that eventually she'd become too difficult for me to lift, carry and properly care for. She was very spastic and stiffened her body often. It was becoming more difficult for me to handle her during these periods. This realization began to plague me more often. We could see that Dana would never be able to walk because even at age two and a half she still couldn't sit up by herself or hold her head up.

She had a special wheelchair to keep her body as straight as possible, but even then she had no head control. She drooled so much that she had to wear a bib. Her head would fall down to her chest, so we had to constantly move her head up to avoid strangulation. This happened every few minutes. Even though she needed constant care, I fought against considering facilities like the ones I'd visited. And although I wanted to believe she recognized me, no real signs affirmed that, either. I had trouble reconciling myself to the truth. I needed to believe that I could personally make a difference for her and that she would know I was her mother and would keep her safe. This much I knew for sure: If we did have to place her, it would never be in dreary surroundings, no matter how long we waited. We'd wait until we could find her a special place with cheerful surroundings and loving caretakers.

As I went back and forth about the idea of placing Dana, my mind played tricks on me. The internal conflicts wreaked havoc. Although I saw her clearly, I still tried to convince myself that her disabilities would not be as severe as I feared they were. By placing her, I would be confirming what others had been telling me, and I was not yet ready to accept that. I'd conjured up an imaginary place, thinking I could place her nearby, in a home away from home. If it didn't happen, if I couldn't find this perfect place, then so be it. I would forever be her caretaker, or so I told myself. After all, she was my child.

# A big change

Interestingly enough, a home away from home is exactly where children with disabilities are living today when they are older or can no longer be physically cared for by their families. They're not abandoned. They can remain as part of the family, something quite different from years ago when parents were much less involved after placing their child. This change resulted from parents playing an active role in the creation of home-like settings for their children, with house mothers/ fathers to watch over the kids. For these children to be able to experience a home setting, someplace they could call their own, took years of parents' determination to break down the resistance of the community.

Finally, when parents became activists and established homes on their own for their children, only then did the professionals begin to listen and ultimately agree that this might be possible. Those with disabilities who could, learned independent living skills, proving that their lives were viable and important, with many becoming contributing members of society. Living away from home when reaching adulthood is a natural developmental step for all people, including those with disabilities. In the case of younger children who are living out of the home, they can still participate with their families whenever they are able. Comments about having "those children" or "those strange-looking people" from residents protesting inclusion of the disabled in their neighborhoods can no longer stand up in court. As a result, even more homes are now available for children and adults with disabilities who need to be independent.

As I was feeling low about the reality of Dana's disability and her future, I was becoming more distressed because I wasn't finding the ideal place I dreamed of. This made for almost a deeper loss than when she was born. When she was born, we had some hope because we didn't know what to expect. Now that our expectations were realistic, we felt less hopeful than before. Even though my dad thought placing Dana would radically improve our life, I couldn't imagine the future without having her in my life.

I remember seeing a Broadway play called "Joe Egg." It was about a single father caring alone for a teenage daughter with severe disabilities. She, like Dana, had CP and couldn't speak. The autobiographical play told of his constant struggle between trying to maintain his own life and job while caring for his daughter. There was a dream sequence in the play that struck close to my heart. The father was napping in a chair on the porch facing his daughter in her wheelchair on a hot summer day. Suddenly, his daughter rose gracefully from her wheelchair and began to dance toward her father, elegantly, like a ballerina. She was so beautiful and graceful as she danced across the stage. She smiled at him in a way she'd never smiled before. Time stopped as the father was mesmerized by her slow and fluid motions. Then he awakened, and realizing this was just a dream, he buried his head into his folded arms and cried mournfully.     That was exactly the way I felt. The scene brought me to tears. I, too, had fantasized about Dana and imagined her without disabilities.

## The second death

If the first death was the loss of my dream, the second was placement and facing the truth about Dana. (The third death, when she physically passed, was more of a coming to peace.)

Just when I was beginning to give up on the idea of finding the ideal home for Dana, my mother's friend told her that a relative of hers had a son in a "wonderful" placed called Hillside House. I'd heard about Hillside House in Santa Barbara, but I was wary of going to yet another place and being disappointed. I was just beginning to accept that Dana was going to be with us, and I sadly began thinking about our plans.

But on a warm Sunday morning, Don and I and Hal and Margie all decided to visit. We left Dana and Mark at home with their respective grandparents. It would be too stressful for everyone to have the kids with us while we were contemplating placement for them.

I couldn't ignore how lovely and colorful Santa Barbara was as it spilled down the hills to the sea. It'd been many years since I'd visited there, and I was struck by how unchanged it seemed, despite the new storefronts and real-estate offices. The Spanish décor of the city was elegantly old, genteel, and very welcoming. It was a bright, sunny day that put me at odds with my feelings.

Because, despite the beauty of the city and the warmth of the day, I began to feel apprehensive even as we approached the town's outskirts. I was holding my breath and dreading every minute as we neared Hillside House. I was acutely afraid of what we were planning to do and where we were headed. I didn't know what to expect.

One thing I did know: I was grateful to have another couple along with the two of us, even though they were as nervous as we. We needed each other's support. I was flooded with feelings of guilt, and wondering: What the hell was I doing? Never before, and never since, have I felt so lost, so unsure, so desperate to find an answer. I wanted to know what to do. I needed a confirmation, something that would tell us where to go, or if we really should turn back.

When we finally arrived at noon, Hillside House was as beautiful as it had been described. I was taken aback. The building was nestled in a park-like setting at the base of foothills, set amid lush, green, wild grass. Mustard covered the hills behind it, illuminating the whole area with a dazzling brightness. How deeply I wished that Don and I and Dana were there for a summer getaway, where we could run freely, have great meals together, and take long hikes into the majestic hillside. But I knew why we were there, and I was dying inside. Was this to be Dana's new home?

That trip to Santa Barbara was so long ago, yet the memory haunts me as I write these words. I thought that Dana's life had come to a dead end. There was no place to go, no education for her, and little therapy to help her improve. She was never going to get better. She would always be like a six-month-old, only larger. I feared that others might judge us for not hanging in there and having her live out her life with us.

In fact, I had difficulty with that issue myself as well. It was unsettling, to say the least. I had to face that I was not the perfect mother, not even close. Lost to me was the dream of being the successful mother who could cope with anything. I could not forgive myself.

## A difficult decision

But we forged on, and two weeks after our initial visit to Hillside House, the four of us, plus Dana and Mark, headed there again. On the way up, we were all very quiet, periodically interrupted by the two kids' vocalizations and high-pitched sounds. We were all deeply involved in our own thoughts. I couldn't stop thinking how much I felt like a failure as a mother, wishing that I could have been more effective for Dana. I also remember feeling both relieved and guilty about making this difficult decision. I came across a quote by William Faulkner that had an impact on me, something that eased my ambivalent feelings: "All of us failed to match our dreams of perfection."

I knew that Dana would be treated with the utmost of care, judging from what I'd seen earlier. Watching the staff deal effortlessly with those children with the most severe disabilities reassured me but also made me once again guilty over the fact that it had been such a struggle for me to hold Dana and feed her while she mostly choked and gagged on the food. At Hillside House were kids just like Dana who needed to be held and spoon-fed, but unlike her, they managed to swallow without incident.

When we arrived with Mark and Dana, they were greeted outside by Mr. Cox, all the staff, and kids. As we unloaded all of the clothes, the staff led us to their respective bedrooms that Dana and Mark each were sharing with three other children. This scene could have been college kids moving into their dorms, except the mood was quite different. We all felt terrible that our two children didn't have a clue as to what was happening. They'd know soon enough, we told ourselves, which was a hard fact to swallow.

After we got them settled, we went to a little inn where we would stay for the weekend. We dropped off our belongings and hurried back. None of us were willing to take our kids to Hillside and then make a quick get-away. For the whole weekend, we stayed at as long as they would allow us. Mr. Cox gave up his weekend to be with us, knowing how difficult this was. We passed the time by talking to the kids, the staff and Mr. Cox. Don and Hal were more philosophical about the separation from our kids, but they were extremely patient with Margie and me.

Several hours later, Mr. Cox gently explained that we needed to leave now and not return for two weeks to allow the kids to adjust to their new home properly. He was kind and gentle in the way that he spoke to us. We knew that our staying any longer would serve no one and would only increase our anxiety, although I don't know how much more anxious I could've felt. Don gently urged me to take Mr. Cox's advice, which, of course, I did. The feeling elicited an image of me clinging onto a cliff by my fingernails, just hanging on for life, not wanting to give up Dana.

My memories of the next week are blurry, but I do know that I called every day to get a progress report from Mr. Cox. Every call was the same. He reassured me that Dana was doing well, eating well, and appeared quite happy. I was never sure whether to believe him. As a mom, I couldn't fully entrust anyone else with caring for my child.

I paid little attention to myself during this whole process of letting go. Other than being aware of my misery, I wasn't at all in touch with my body, except for suddenly realizing I hadn't had my period that month. Don and I had always agreed, from the very beginning, that we wanted a family. But we were so consumed by Dana and the events surrounding her life and placement that we didn't consciously think of having a baby now, not at this time.

# Good news, bad news

By the time we saw Dana after the two-week waiting period, I did, in fact, discover that I was pregnant. I had a sudden flashback of that evening when we told our parents that Don was drafted and that we were about to have a baby. It was ironic that now when we were placing Dana, I would discover that I was pregnant once again. Good news, bad news. Timing is everything.

My feelings were mixed. Mostly, I felt real fear about going through pregnancy and another birth and guilt about Dana. While my greatest fears were centered on having a healthy baby and concerned that Dana wouldn't be replaced by our new child, I couldn't help feeling joy about having another chance.

My thoughts were crazy as I pondered the prospect of this new child and whether this baby would be healthy, and how he or she would feel about Dana. I also wondered if it was going to be a boy or girl, but I knew that it didn't really matter. I thought about what kind of mother I would be and then I hoped the child would live a long, productive life. I was getting another chance! We might even become grandparents some day! And I realized that I could never, ever go through what I'd just endured with Dana.

As the months went on, I struggled with missing Dana and the fact she was no longer in our home. I would enter her room at night and look at the hand-painted wallpaper picturing three little girls dressed in old-fashioned dresses. It was paper I'd selected right after she was born.

Seeing her bed empty, I felt deeply depressed during the following six months before the new baby came. Instead of feeling joyful, I couldn't stop worrying. Nothing had been as it was supposed to be. How could I anticipate joy?

I couldn't allow myself to feel anything freely, other than relief that Dana was making a good adjustment. Within a few months, the staff was able to feed her without taking as long as before. She was finally becoming more able to swallow and digest solid food.

I could hardly believe that my daughter, who could not suck at birth, was now eating regular food. While it was a relief to know that she could now tolerate more than baby food, I still felt ambivalent. It was upsetting to know that I could not advance her to this stage, but gratifying to know that they could feed her. I had no idea what prevented me from getting her to eat, but upset as I was, I felt grateful to the Hillside House staff for sticking with it and succeeding. I was so appreciative of their dedication to Dana and to all the children there.

Meanwhile, my pregnancy was advancing, and we regularly visited Dana every two to three weeks. I'd bring her new clothes each visit as a way to help me feel more involved as her mother, but our visits left me feeling bereft. I told myself that she knew Don and me, but in reality, she didn't. It's difficult to have a meaningful relationship with a child who neither knows you nor responds to you. The thing that kept us going was our friendly relationship with the older kids and taking Dana on outings to the beach or to a park.

As the years progressed, Dana remained as she was at birth—sweet, unresponsive, and hampered by severe motor impairments. She was never able to sit and hold her head up independently. One day when we were visiting her, I was terribly shocked to find her hair all cut off in a very unbecoming, boyish style. It'd been done without our knowledge.

I'd always loved to brush her beautiful soft, blond hair, which I kept at a medium length. The staffers hadn't considered asking our permission but simply cut it because they decided she'd be easier to care for with short hair. I couldn't believe they did that! They weren't treating her like a person in her own right.

Even though I knew it made no difference to her, I felt as if I was no longer Dana's mother in the eyes of the Hillside staff. I was crestfallen. It seemed to me that they were in charge and we'd lost her. They simply did it for convenience, without thinking about how we would feel. It was as if she had become a thing, not a person. Although we were upset, we said nothing. We kept up our hope for a few years that she might improve and eventually come home. But Mr. Cox gently persuaded us that her disabilities were too severe to allow her to come home. I wondered how he knew that? What if *she* knew differently? We would never know.

## Trepidation, courage, and joy!

As the time approached for our baby to be born, we left nothing unturned. This time, with complete cooperation from a new doctor, our child would be born on April 8, two weeks before the actual due date. I was to enter the hospital the night before and have a caesarean the next morning. I was not to go into labor. Of course, I couldn't help feeling nervous as I waited.

A nurse on staff came in with a blood-pressure cuff and said, "Let's have a look at how your BP is doing." She fitted the device on my arm, pumped it up, and waited. When the numbers appeared, she turned on her heels and ran out of the room. "What's wrong?" I cried, but she was gone and I was scared.

However, she returned shortly with a hospital staff doctor who told me, "Gayle, your systolic blood pressure is 250. That's way, way too high. What's going on here?"

I told her about Dana and how nervous I was about my child's impending birth, but that I otherwise felt perfectly fine. Upon further examination, the doctor reassured me. "Your excessively high blood pressure appears to have more to do with your level of stress than the state of your health. I feel confident you're O.K., but we need to monitor your blood pressure very closely. Understand?" I did, of course.

And this time, events did go smoothly. I was finally convinced that my new doctor (after I told him about our previous horror story) was going to handle the situation differently. In the short three and a half years since Dana's birth, progress seemed to have been made in terms of physicians listening to their patients. Or in our case the improvement was due to a new informed doctor, a different hospital, and a wiser mother. In any event, a healthy son, Scott, was born.

Although Don was still not allowed to participate in Scott's birth, as dads are now encouraged to do, he immediately joined me in the delivery room right after the caesarean delivery. I was groggy from the local anesthetic but aware enough to know that Don was there with me to share in the joy of Scott's birth. Things were so different from the first time. The doctor included us in every step of Scott's birth. There were to be no surprises. The medical staff seemed relaxed and happy. Scott had a momentary blip in that he was a bit blue after birth, but quickly regained a healthy, rosy hue within seconds. I knew at that moment that everything was going to be fine.

As soon as I left the recovery room, the nurse brought this tiny little bundle to me. I remember she was holding him upright on her hand and I couldn't help noticing how he was holding his little head very high with his dark eyes gazing intently at me. She handed him to me and said cheerfully, "Here's your little football player!"

As much as I didn't want to compare, I couldn't help remembering Dana at three weeks old, her gaze listless and her body wound so tight. Now I understood the difference between a healthy child and one who'd suffered a birth trauma. Although only a few hours old, this little baby boy had more strength and agility than his sister did at age three and a half

Our prayers had been answered. We had another chance to raise a healthy child.

## The perfect child

As he grew up, Scott proved to be a funny and interesting boy, always coming up with surprising commentaries. Don and I did everything to encourage his development. To be honest, I went overboard to stimulate him with puzzles, games and anything that would promote his development. In addition, Don spent time participating with and encouraging Scott's athletic activities, even as a very young child. He was swimming independently before he was two.

# Confronting the Second Death

On some level we understood that Scott had to be the child that Dana could never be, the perfect child. We couldn't help it at the time. I guess I unconsciously needed to do it right this time. I'm sure this put an inordinate amount of pressure on him, even though he seemed to relish challenges in learning and competing.

He was like a little sponge, taking in all that the world had to offer. It's difficult to assess just how much Dana's disability played into Scott's growing up. Somehow I believe that he felt that he had to make up for Dana by achieving and by trying to please us. Although he's had a successful life, I believe that's come at a cost to him vis-à-vis Dana. He visited her at Hillside House only a few times because we were advised by professionals then not to "expose" her too much to him. They felt he would be somehow compromised by feelings of fear, guilt, or lack of understanding, so different from the advice given today.

I believe he escaped those feelings. Scott felt something toward Dana, but it wasn't guilt. He appeared curious and not particularly upset when he visited her. If he felt anything, it was sadness for her. He told me recently that he never felt worried about becoming disabled or incapacitated. We made sure that Scott, and later our daughter Heidi, understood as much as they could about her. Watching us interact with Dana made Scott feel more secure. He later told us that he remembered how touched he was by our sweet and gentle interactions with her, but realized, even at his young and tender age, that she didn't know us.

Nevertheless, it was pretty obvious that he did think about her often because when he was around three years old, he would introduce himself to others and exclaim, in all seriousness, "Hi, my name is Scott, and I have a sister who is handiwrapped!"

He was a funny little kid, who made people laugh with this comment, but who knows how he really felt?

Life went on pretty smoothly, and we continued to visit Dana but not as frequently. After visiting briefly with Dana, Don would leave me to be with her while he would take Scott, and eventually Heidi, on outings to the beach or to the park. It never was easy for Don to be with Dana for very long, which I understood and—finally—accepted.

## Off limits

The entire time that Dana lived away, only my parents would periodically visit Dana with us. It was apparent that our family and friends considered Hillside House off limits and the matter of Dana handled. We never thought too much of this; probably Margie and Hal were going through the same thing. Except for their daughter, Leslie, and Margie's mother, no other family members or friends visited either. Having Margie and Hal close by to experience the same ordeal sustained us sufficiently to deal with our situation. The lack of visits to Dana by other family members was never brought up, discussed, or even expected, nor do I ever remember considering this consciously. I think that attitudes in those days were less sophisticated and a child with a disability was generally not accepted in society, and placement was expected.

Placement of children out of home then meant the end of the line. Consequently, when Dana left home, she was gone forever, but not as far as I was concerned, which is probably why Dana strongly influenced my life's work. I needed to keep her alive and important in a special way. Though that motive wasn't conscious, it served its purpose: Dana's life came to have meaning for all children.

In those early days, parents of children with disabilities felt as if they were second-class citizens but wouldn't challenge those who made them feel that way. They didn't have the rights that parents have now. I was determined to change all that. As a family therapist, I worked hard to show parents they could achieve what they wanted for their children, and together, we succeeded. I couldn't help but remember the feelings of failure I experienced, and now I had a chance to help others abandon the misery that I and so many others experienced. As the Irish critic Edward Dowden wrote, "Sometimes a noble failure serves the world as faithfully as a distinguished success."

## A Valentine's baby

When Scott was almost four, on February 14, 1963, our second daughter, Heidi, was born, healthy and beautiful. Our Valentine's baby! Both pregnancies subsequent to Dana were fraught with tremendous worry and anxiety, fears that another catastrophe would ensue. But the moment Heidi was born, we knew she was perfect.

During our stay in the hospital, our pediatrician rushed over to see newborn Heidi at the request of my father (unbeknownst to me), who panicked when he thought she had tremors. Tremors were on our minds, naturally. All of our nerves were understandably on edge, including the pediatrician's. But when the doctor saw Heidi in the hospital, he reassured my dad and us that all newborns have tremors from time to time and that they soon would subside. He told my dad, "She couldn't be healthier." My dad apologized and said, "I'm sorry to have alarmed everyone, doctor, but we just couldn't help worrying."

Our approach at home with Heidi was far more relaxed from Day 1. I couldn't believe how comparatively easy it was to raise two young children. I used up all of my strength and energy with Dana from the very beginning. I was always in a tense state with her. But with Scott and Heidi, I was relaxed and free from anguish.

By now we recognized that we did not need to have the perfect child and that Heidi didn't have to be an overachiever for us. I felt much more confident than I did with Dana and even with Scott. Finally, as with Scott, I held her and cuddled her as much as I could. It took no effort to make the kids laugh. I was so grateful.

# Typical behavior

Heidi was different than Scott because she was a little more sensitive and experienced hurt feelings more often. She also had very strong opinions, ranging from what she wanted to wear to what she wanted to do. She took everything to heart and also wanted very much to be like her big brother. Scott and Heidi had the typical sibling jealousies and acted them out from time to time, which would get on our nerves but never enough to make us crazy. Secretly, I was grateful for their typical behaviors.

Heidi, as a young child, didn't outwardly express any thoughts about Dana, but she, like Scott, was curious when she visited her sister. Heidi told me recently that she remembers visiting Dana when Heidi was around six years old. When Heidi saw Dana, she perceived her older sister as a younger child, much smaller and frailer than herself. In actuality, Heidi was very petite and about the same size as Dana. Although Dana was seven years older than Heidi, Heidi's reaction was clearly colored by the severity of Dana's disability.

Both Heidi and Scott speak of Dana with tenderness, even though their relationship with her was limited. The earliest recollection Scott has of Dana is remembering when Dana came home to visit one summer when Scott was about three and a half. He recalls Don and me, when the visit was over, driving away with Dana and feeling sad that she had to leave. He also remembers some adult explaining to him that we were taking Dana to her real home. He must have felt upset and curious why his sister's real home wasn't where he and Heidi lived.

## Dana's Death

Time moved along briskly for our family until the summer of 1969 when Mr. Cox called me from Hillside House to say that Dana wasn't doing well. There was no real diagnosis, only evidence that her condition was beginning to worsen. After he broke this news, I must've held the phone receiver for five minutes before I could speak. The feared reality was now approaching. Her time on this earth was ending. As Mr. Cox kept talking to me gently, I couldn't say anything. The familiar lump in my throat returned. I knew that the time was here, but she was only 14½ years old. I wasn't ready. It was too soon!

Dr. Janss's words from many years before went through my mind—"children with severe disabilities like Dana tend to die young, usually around puberty." I should've known this would happen. But we'd felt so comfortable knowing Dana was doing well at Hillside House that we put aside the possibility that she would actually die so young. All of us lived in a cocoon when it came to facing that terrible realization.

The worst part was that I could do nothing about it. As much as I was dreadfully afraid to see her in a bad condition, we went to see her. Although she didn't appear as ill as I thought she would, Mr. Cox confirmed that this really was the beginning of the end, based on her vital signs. We visited her and watched her become frailer. She was skin and bones. My heart felt dead. It was six months before the end really came. They found her in bed one morning after she had apparently suffered a heart attack, although they were never really sure. That was September, 1970. She was not quite 14½.

My reaction to her death was strange: real sadness, but not as deep of a heart ache as when we placed her. When we placed her, I felt I'd really lost her. I grieved then as one would have grieved a death. I mourned all the things in her life that she couldn't do. I grieved over the loss of a relationship that I wished I could've had with her.

But after she actually died, I realized that her death relieved me of the terrible anguish I felt for her. When she died, I'd had difficulty justifying her life. I couldn't grasp what the point was of her living such a painful life? Why did she have to suffer? I was so embittered about the whole experience that I never wanted to see or hear the word "disability" again.

As a result of the pain, the agony and grief, I was determined that this part of my life was closed; the pages were sealed and were never to be reopened. I needed to go on and do all the normal things I thought everyone else did. The agony and suffering would be over, I decided.

## *It takes time*

As I focused on Scott and Heidi, I thought it was going to be so much simpler raising them than Dana. It was easier in a sense, but certainly no cakewalk. For years following their births, an underlying fear nagged at me that something terrible could happen to them. Rather than think that we'd paid our dues and that God wouldn't punish us again by harming our children, I thought just the opposite. I felt very vulnerable, as if trouble were waiting around the corner.

For some time, I felt that what I held special and dear could be wrenched away at any time. When things were going too well, I worried that something bad might happen to Don and our kids. I knew it was irrational, but I couldn't get over the feelings of precipitous doom. At least I knew enough to keep my feelings to myself and not show them my fears.

Fortunately, my husband was more stable in that arena and helped me dispel my irrational fantasies. My guess is that those fantasies lingered as long as my guilt feelings over my inability to care for Dana. Thankfully, I changed over the years and came to realize that difficulties happen to everyone, and they happen neither in any particular order nor for any particular reason.

The good and the bad memories shape us and remain a part of us. We learn to handle what comes to us as best we can, and some of us do that better than others. Focusing on a negative future, I learned, is self-defeating. Of course, most of my fears that bad things laid in wait for us never materialized. I can't imagine how I'd be now if I'd stayed in that place, always fearful and projecting that fear the future. Who knows what I would have become? Although some of our experiences are filled with fear, pain, and trauma, we must rely on our powers of intellect and spirit to overcome our negativity. We mustn't shut down and become permanently defeated. There's always a solution. It just takes time.

When Dana was born with disabilities, I felt defeated as though I had no solutions or choices. This left me feeling anxious, hopeless, and depressed. I thought the world had come to an end. Although this is understandable, the danger lies in the ongoing feeling that we can never regain our power. This happens often in people who experience severe trauma, and if the feeling of powerlessness lasts for too long, they can end up feeling paralyzed. My life seemed so bleak that I couldn't see that I had any power to choose anything in my life, until I went into therapy.

"It's not what happens to you," Viktor Frankl said famously, "it's what you do about what happens to you." In other words, while we can't usually help what happens to us, if we learn to face ourselves honestly and objectively, in time we can regain our inner strength. Life is not static; things change. What we feel today will undoubtedly be very different tomorrow. It took a lot of years for me to believe that and trust that I was powerful. I began to listen to my inner self and trust my instincts, which have carried me through to this day. As Scott and Heidi were growing up, I really learned to become resilient and to appreciate what was good in my life rather than to allow myself to become beaten down by the negative stuff. Slowly, the negativity gave way to the positive affirmations.

## Growing up

Heidi and Scott's growing up was pretty typical but certainly not perfect. I was grateful to have two healthy kids, a fact I finally began to accept. Like most families, our kids had their own difficulties, some more troublesome than others. We considered ourselves fortunate that their challenges mostly centered on typical problems, like self-esteem issues, growing up, and being accepted. Sometimes friends would run roughshod over them, which was tough, but manageable. We never lost sight of the fact that things could always be a lot worse.

As kids, both were pretty hard on themselves and self-demanding. Mostly, they were good students and responsible kids. Scott was often funny, mugging and cracking jokes, but serious when he had to be. Even Heidi could not resist his funny antics at times and would join him in the fun. They would become a comedy team and recite scripts word for word from funny movies, which would bring Don and me to mirthful tears. We so appreciated their healthy lives, and were thankful that both turned out to be kind, industrious, and good people.

Heidi said she would've liked an older sister as an ally to protect her from her big brother when they would fight. She needed a sister she could relate to, one with whom to share things. She regretted that Dana couldn't be the sister she desired. At times, I took their problems too much to heart, and I had to force myself to remember that no matter how difficult their lives could be, Heidi and Scott were healthy and would eventually work out their problems as best they could.

As they grew, Don and I earnestly tried to keep the lines of communication open between them and us, so that we could be available during tough times. We wanted to help our kids as much as we could, but we realized that wasn't always possible. While I would find myself too consumed with their problems and worried about their struggles, Don often took a more casual approach. I finally relaxed my fears after Heidi, at 18, said to me one day, "Mom, all you need to do is to listen to me. You don't have to always try to fix my problems."

I knew she was right, and I thanked her for letting me off the hook. I realize now that my anxiety over my children stemmed from my inability to "fix" Dana, which I didn't understand until Heidi freed me. Don reminds me, even today, that there exists in me, some of my father, who always wanted to fix things for his family.

Heidi was entitled to deal with her own problems and have her privacy. All I wanted for my kids was to be their rock, their support. I guess I desired everything to be perfect for them. But how could they manage their lives if I was so busy trying to fix their problems? Who needed whom? Both kids made me realize that I wasn't perfect, nor did I have to be, which turned out to be relief. What a good teacher Heidi was! Her wisdom gave me great cause to reflect.

Both managed to deal with their problems as best they could, and although some of their challenges left battle scars, the scars belonged to them and not to me. These did not appear to be permanent disfigurements. Looking back, I'm grateful my kids caused me to step back and not rob them of their ability to handle their own lives.

Scott and Heidi went on to college and graduate schools, and then married. Scott has a daughter, Sammy, who's now 12½. Heidi and her husband Steve have two sons, Matthew and Daniel, ages 11 and seven. The three healthy grandkids have been a great bonus for Don and me. As they grow older, they're getting busier with school and activities, but every year on the Memorial Day weekend, we take the three on a grand tour of a great American city, without their parents. It's something we all treasure.

Heidi and Steve are celebrating their 21st anniversary. Scott, divorced from Sammy's mother, remarried a wonderful woman, Candice, who brings with her three more children, increasing the family fun. There's always room for more!

While there have been rocky moments for Scott and Sammy and Heidi and Steve, generally joyful periods have dominated. And in all of their lives, Don and I remain grateful observers and willing participants.

Chapter 6

# Finding My Calling

"I slept and dreamed that life was joy. I awoke and saw that life was service acted and behold, service was joy."

—*Rabindrnath Tagore*

*A* year after Dana's death, our lives became more "normal," but I felt a deep need to do something significant. I was beginning to notice that I saw myself as a victim, a role I quickly became tired of. Instead, I felt compelled to give back to society by becoming involved in some meaningful volunteerism or occupation, but in a way that balanced my availability to my kids and to Don.

Scott and Heidi were becoming more independent. My need to contribute was different from the role my mother chose. She put her family and social life above all, but I saw that I didn't want her life. She became terribly depressed when my brother and I married within two months of each other. All the meaning seemed to go out of my mother's existence when we left home. Watching her struggle with this "empty-nest syndrome" left a deep impression on me and unconsciously spurred me on to different ambitions.

# Volunteering

I began to volunteer in various activities, but nothing really spoke to me. I'd always been fascinated by medicine, but never felt I had the perseverance needed to become a physician. I would often sit with my uncle (the orthopedist) as a young child and watch movies of his surgeries, which I loved. So when I had the opportunity to volunteer in a hospital as an orthopedic aide, I took it. While I enjoyed being in a hospital environment, the volunteer work itself wasn't particularly satisfying because I was doing mostly errands.

Later, I volunteered in a probation department as a mentor to a young teenage girl. Her father was in jail, and her mother was a drug addict with little time or ability to care for her. I became the girl's friend as I coached her several times a week. I enjoyed helping her, and she valued having someone to talk to. In fact, it was the first time that anyone had ever taken time to show her any interest. I was very proud when she decided to break away from a potential life of petty crime. This gave me great satisfaction, but it wasn't my calling.

The next opportunity was working as a Spanish-speaking paraprofessional counselor in a managed-care hospital. There I helped poor Hispanic families cope with all sorts of problems. I learned so much and began to feel fulfilled and needed. After being supervised by psychotherapists, I felt this was something I might pursue. Seeing the positive results in the families I counseled encouraged me to search out the field of psychology as a possible field of study.

At the same time I entered a year-long certificate program at UCLA that focused on developing one's potential. Women at that point were just beginning to take themselves more seriously. They were interested in finding and developing their talents, and many decided to go back to school. This class was designed to help the student identify his or her specific areas of interest and talent. Although this class was open to all, everyone in it was female. The program helped me discover my talent as a potential psychotherapist and shape a direction for me to pursue.

Shortly thereafter, a social-worker friend approached me about volunteering at the UCLA Early Infant/Toddler Program for children with disabilities. Coincidentally, this was the same program Dana had attended many years before. My friend suggested that because of my personal experience with Dana, I could be very helpful to the parents whose children attended the program.

How ironic! I discovered that the medical director of the program was still Dr. Janss, the wonderful pediatrician who worked with Dana for two years. We met and we hugged, but before she gave permission for me to volunteer, she wanted me to speak with a few parents in the program to see if they were interested in working with me. It was hard to believe that barely a year and a half had passed since Dana's death when I'd sworn never again to deal with disability. But here I was considering helping other parents of children with disabilities cope with their situation. Go figure.

## Dana's legacy

My instincts spoke loud and clear to me: "This is a very important opportunity, take it!" I prayed that Dr. Janss would allow me in after I spoke with the parents. Here's where the years of pain and sorrow could channel negative energy into strength and healing not only for me, but also for other parents like me. This was the real beginning that nurtured the seed of Dana's legacy for thousands of others, although I didn't know it at the time.

I spoke to the parents about my experiences with Dana. Mostly, they wanted to know how I felt as I went through her years of life and death and how I dealt with her. Talking to them was very helpful for them and, especially, for me. And it gave us a chance to be open with each other. I saw a tremendous need inside the parents to communicate and learn more from each other. They'd never shared their feelings with anyone else. I found myself awestruck by the experience. A sense of healing stirred within me.

They asked to meet again, and Dr. Janss approved, but on a limited basis. The parents met together weekly, behind the one-way mirror, to talk and try to make sense of what they felt were senseless situations. For the first time, they could converse with other parents like themselves.

## A hub

I could see that Dana's life could be the answer to helping these parents move from heartbreak to healing. Unwittingly, this legacy unfolded and became ongoing and one that has become a hub around which my life turned. This is where I belonged. I never would've known I'd be in Dana's debt in so many ways, large and small.

I met with Dr. Janss periodically to discuss how I might be of help to the parents who brought their children to the program.

Knowing the precarious process that parents go through when discovering their child has a disability, I felt I could help them avoid certain pitfalls that many parents experience. I wanted to assure them that they weren't alone, especially because I'd felt so alone at the beginning of my journey. As my friend the social worker and I thought, parents who have support and an open forum to exchange their feelings and ideas will feel less isolated and become much more effective in their parenting and in their lives.

It was my hope they'd gain strength and knowledge from each other. This thinking grew from my personal journey, my experiential learning, rather than from formal teaching or from any theoretical framework. I had to learn on the job because no psychology programs existed to deal with the emotional aspects of parents and their children with disabilities. I learned as much as I could informally from the parents we were in contact with.

No support groups existed, nor were parents involved in the assessment or support of their children's needs. Mostly, they had to rely on the doctor for everything, but that usually didn't include emotional support. The physicians assessed the children's problems by mostly identifying what was wrong with particular body parts. The whole child—let alone the child as part of a family—was barely considered. These parents were frightened about their child's disability, but their burning questions were seldom addressed.

Dr. Janss, being progressive, understood the plight of the parents, and seemed to like the idea of having me there. We talked about having me meet with parents for the hour and a half or so while they waited for their children who were participating in the program. The doctor felt the children would make more progress if the parents were less stressed. She and I agreed it was important for parents to have an outlet for communication and a safe place for sharing so they could begin to relax and cope more effectively.

It'd been years since Dana had attended the UCLA program, seemingly a different lifetime. Yet, sitting in that familiar room where parents observed their children, brought back feelings I thought were buried in the past. Moms sat in the small room, chatting quietly as they watched, through a one-way mirror, therapists working with their children, just as we had done years before. Nothing much had changed.

## The journey begins

Then and there I began my journey of helping others. I wasn't yet aware what an impact this would have on me, but I know now that I healed each day through the gift of helping others. In fact, it's a journey that continues. Today, 40 years later, I continue to run a parent group whose roots began at UCLA's program.

On my first day as the new parent-support volunteer leader (unofficial title) at the UCLA Intervention Program, I told them about Dana and that Dr. Janss agreed that I might be helpful to them. The hour and a half went by so quickly, and they asked if I could return again. They hoped I would serve as a mentor, helping them understand and deal with their challenges. Specifically, they hoped I could help them learn to communicate more effectively with the physicians and therapists as well as other family members, including their children and spouses. They'd never before had the opportunity to share themselves in this manner with someone who had lived their life and knew their journey.

Although Dr. Janss had supported the idea wholeheartedly, she guardedly granted permission for me to meet on a regular, but limited, basis with the parents. She wanted to be sure that I was responsible and capable enough to do the job well. Because I wasn't a professional counselor, she was naturally protective of the parents. I had to prove myself as worthy to her as well as to the parents.

The program had a dozen or so children in the morning program and another dozen in the afternoon. Each program ran three hours, although some parents did not stay for the whole period. I volunteered in the morning program. As a trial, we met twice weekly for two months. Eventually, the parents would stay for these parent sessions instead of just dropping their child off and leaving.

Dr. Janss was naturally mindful of the parents' reactions and requested that I write notes regarding our meetings. The moms felt encouraged by the sessions and agreed to my taking notes, but without the use of names for their sake of privacy.

The groups proved to be very successful, and I gained the parents' trust unequivocally. It was the only Los Angeles parent group of its kind at that time. It was open to all parents of children attending the program, and most participated. Other groups would meet to hear speakers or meet for reasons other than sharing personal issues.

Our group eventually became very close. I remained as a volunteer at UCLA, meeting twice weekly for almost three years, predominantly with the moms, though occasionally dads would show up, too. As time passed, the members' willingness to speak more openly grew as they began to trust each other.

As part of the process, Dr. Janss invited me to some of the clinics (case meetings) where specialists met with the child and his or her parents to discuss the child's case. It was very helpful for me to learn more about each child so I'd have a deeper connection with the parents as they talked about their child. I was very happy in this role as a volunteer and could have continued on for years helping the parents...until an unforeseen event occurred.

Dr. Janss decided to retire at the beginning of my third year in 1974. I, along with everyone else, was surprised and disappointed. We'd all come to rely on her. She was the backbone of the UCLA program, and everyone dreaded her leaving. Who could possibly take this icon's place? The parents, however, appeared to take this news in stride, feeling that Dr. Janss had put in so much effort for so many years that she deserved to take time for herself. Although their children's disabilities still existed and had to be carefully managed, the parents felt less anxious and more confident in their own interactions with the physicians.

They were also feeling better about themselves and their children. They had faith that Dr. Janss would find them another experienced doctor who'd be able to carry on well for their children. The groups had provided the parents a sense of confidence, making them realize that they, not just the doctors, were the key for their children. They would miss Dr. Janss and viewed her as an important part of their child's life, but they knew she was no longer the major element.

The parents, grateful and loyal to her and to the program, became active fundraisers for the UCLA program, which always was in need of money. This not only helped the programs, but also gave the parents energy and a sense of gratification that they were able to give back to the wonderful place that had helped their children.

## On my way out...and up

Dr. Janss brought in a new, young, developmental pediatrician to take her place. Following in her footsteps had to be a most difficult task for anyone. Though Dr. Janss left as the program's medical director, she served as a consultant to children and their families for many years thereafter. Dr. Janss had developed confidence in me because the parents told her how helpful I'd been for them. Naturally, I expected things would carry on as always, but to my chagrin, I was wrong. The new doctor, not surprisingly, had her own ideas about running the intervention program. She felt I had too much responsibility as a nonprofessional in counseling the parents, so she hired a brand-new social worker in order to have a professional staff person present.

Although I understood the doctor's intentions, the social worker she hired had no children and no experience with children with disabilities. I realized that this young, talented doctor had to step into the shoes of an icon and was probably nervous about it and even more worried about having a paraprofessional staff person. The social worker came on feeling immediately threatened and resentful of my position with the parents. It was clear to her and to me that she felt out of her league, bewildered, and not knowing exactly what to do. She especially didn't understand the parents' feelings.

For obvious reasons, she didn't want anyone to know this and covered it over with arrogance. The parents sensed this and were very unhappy with her patronizing ways, so they complained to the doctor. The social worker had her own ideas, which clearly did not fit with theirs. At the same time, she was complaining bitterly to the doctor about me behind my back. She had told me it was no longer necessary for me to go to the clinics now that she was there. This apparently was not true because the new physician still expected me to continue, but I didn't know that at the time. The dissension was mounting because she clearly wanted me out of the picture.

## The beginning of the end

The parents were showing their resentment, and I could see that this was the beginning of the end for me. Everything that'd been accomplished with the parents was quickly unraveling. The parents were not coming to the group meetings because they felt the social worker had an agenda different from theirs and wasn't interested in their circumstances.

I then knew I would probably have to leave even though I didn't want to. There was clearly room for only one person, and I was not the professional. Despite the parents' pleas to keep me on as the group's facilitator, the doctor decided to "fire" me, even though I was unpaid. But something she said to me had a significant impact on my life. It was in April that she asked me to leave by June because the social worker was coming back from vacation then, she said, and it would be a smoother transition for everyone.

I decided it'd be impossible for me to stay any longer, feeling as badly as I did. I replied, "If I'm not wanted in June, why would you want me to stay now?" With that, she sarcastically replied, "Do what you want, that's the prerogative of a volunteer!" It was at that stunning moment that I realized that if I wanted to continue working and helping parents, then I had to pursue formal training and education. The work with the parents was too important for me to walk away from what I loved.

## Acting oddly

I recognized that this had to be my life's work. But how was I going to get credentialed when I'd only graduated high school and had to return not only to college but to graduate school as well? For someone who'd declared never to think about or mention the word "disability," I was certainly acting oddly. Now, I was devastated that I might never be able to accomplish what I wanted. Working with families and their children with disabilities had become all-important and the most gratifying experience for me, next to having Scott and Heidi. Now, I was alarmed at the possibility of not continuing. It was fine working as a volunteer, but now I knew I must become professional and do it seriously. Could I succeed?

When the new doctor had spoken harshly to me, I was truly dismayed. I feared that all that'd been accomplished would be lost, that the headway that parents had made would disappear and that we'd now return to the old medical model, with parents again relegated to their inferior roles. The parents had come a long way in feeling better about their situations and in developing better relationships with the doctors who earlier ignored them. That brought back the memory of when I was treated as only the "wheels"—the transportation for Dana to her medical appointments—and nothing more.

I sold the parents short, however, because once they gained their new-found power, they weren't about to let go. It wasn't long before they formed a mutually strong and respectful relationship with the new young doctor, and soon she realized children do not live in a vacuum. She learned to value the importance of the family as part of the treatment for the child with a disability.

Although it certainly didn't feel like it at the time, this new young doctor did me a great favor. I felt so strongly about helping families and their children that I knew I had to move forward, despite my fears. Going back to school to become a professional in the field of psychology would provide the training and give me the license to support the families and to create the holistic environment that I knew was critical for the health of the entire family.

After I left the UCLA program in April, I received a phone call from the new doctor's assistant, a serious and kind young man, who invited me to lunch. I thought that was strange, but I was curious enough to go. The reason for lunch was for the doctor to send an apology via her assistant. He was most embarrassed because the doctor had found out after I'd left that the social worker had lied about me, making all sorts of dishonest claims. I'll forego the rest of the details, but I did tell her assistant that although I appreciated the doctor's apology, I wished that she would've spoken to me personally rather than to send him to do her job. Apparently, the parents went to her complaining about the progress they'd made and subsequently lost as a result of the social worker's disinterest and inability to understand their circumstances. Soon, the social worker was asked to leave.

# Back to school

The idea of going to college absolutely terrified me. I wasn't sure I had the intellectual ability or even the stamina to start on that long road. I was 38 years old and knew I would be facing a real challenge because I had to start at the beginning, from undergraduate school all the way through graduate school. It was almost too overwhelming to think about. My insecurity was raging because I was stepping out of my comfort zone.

I was one of many women returning to school, some of whom were looking for a way out of their marriages. Gaining momentum, the women's rights movement was having a strong effect on women who'd previously stayed home and taken care of their children. It was an era when many women felt like second-class citizens in their relationships and wanted more out of their lives.

I felt differently, but I understood their circumstances. They were giving up security for an unknown future. Being single and without support was frightening to them, but they saw education as a chance for a new life and profession.

By contrast, I knew what I wanted and had very definite goals. I wasn't looking for a way out of my life with Don. I knew I could count on him to be supportive of my returning to school wherever it would lead, just as he had been supportive of all my endeavors.

One of the old, fine Catholic women's colleges in Los Angeles, Immaculate Heart College, was establishing a new program for adults, especially women, who wanted to return to school to develop new careers. The nuns were extremely progressive and ahead of their time. For instance, they traded in their habits for conservative sweaters and skirts.

I remember sitting in the office and listening to the dynamic nun in charge of the program. She was most welcoming and very ardent in reassuring me that my fears were unfounded. She told me that I wasn't so dissimilar from others who were thinking about entering the program. "Everyone feels a little anxious entering school after so many years out of school," she said. "After your experience helping the children and their families, you have much to offer and will do fine." I'd been out of school for 20 years, but the nun very gently persuaded me to take the leap. With all that I had gone through in the past, you might think this would've been an easy decision. But, in fact, this felt like the biggest risk I would ever take.

## Entering new territory

As a young girl growing up, I'd had few expectations placed on me. But now I was entering new territory: a potential academic and professional. I was terrified of having to prove myself. I had a recurring dream of being on a high diving board and someone blocking my way, preventing me from going back down the ladder. There wasn't any other way down but to dive, making me feel as if that would be the biggest plunge I'd ever take. Sounds strange, doesn't it? But the dream's message was clear:

I needed to pursue this if I was ever going to achieve what I wanted. And my instincts were to trust that message.

Before I knew it I was immersed in what proved to be one of the most challenging and satisfying periods of my life. In five years, I'd completed my undergraduate and graduate work. I learned to listen to my instincts and follow them. In fact, I got much better at taking risks. After all, nothing is more satisfying than stretching yourself beyond your presumed capabilities and then coming out on top. There I was in a completely different setting with people whom I never would've met, facing challenges together in new and different ways. It was a most exciting time for me.

Several key women of that era in the early '70s visited our campus and left lasting impressions as they spoke of new roles for women. By the time I graduated, many more women of all ages were returning to higher education. Those times will always hold fond memories for me.

It didn't matter that my parents wanted me to stay home and take care of the kids. My folks were still stuck in that old mindset about women, despite the reality that over time the kids need you less and less. I was beyond feeling that I had to explain to my parents that I had no intention of relinquishing care for my children. I'd be home when they were home. I'd attend school when they were in school. I understood that my parents were caught up in that era's stigma: What would people think of their daughter abandoning her family and going to school? Why must she be looking for outside interests? Why did she have to work, after all?

What mattered was how I felt and, secondarily, how proud my husband and children were because of my accomplishment. The support of my children and my husband was most important to me.

## A phenomenal experience

My journey through education was a special time for Don and the kids as well because the house was often filled with my fellow students and teachers. My colleagues and I participated in social gatherings, study groups, and lectures, something quite different from our usual home life. All in all, it wasn't a problem managing my time, caring for my family, and handling the rigors of school. In fact, I loved every minute.

My primary goal was to earn a psychology degree, with the hopes of counseling parents of children with disabilities. However, the thought did occur to me that my new educational experience could lead me down another path. I tried to remain open to all the possibilities. Yet, my original goal stayed with me, and my final thesis project proved that correct.

We had to prepare for orals as part of our final thesis in graduate school. In addition to the orals, I decided on an experiment that might be provocative and answer questions for me as well. Although it'd been proven at UCLA that support groups for parents of children with disabilities were helpful for parents, I wanted to learn how this might affect people who had no relationship at all to the disabled.

So I designed two interactive groups consisting of my fellow students and assigned them roles as parents of children with varying disabilities, based on my case studies with children from the UCLA program. There was no written script, names were changed, and situations were described that involved characteristic families and their relationships.

Before the group process began, I described to the participants the varying emotions that parents went through while raising their children and suggested experiences they might have. The students took this idea and ran with it. The more they became involved in their roles, the more they resembled the parents I'd known. None of us knew where this was going to lead. But the mothers in the group expressed things like the mothers I listened to. The fathers ranged from interested and broken-hearted to disinterested and depressed. I was the facilitator and observer as my fellow students became immersed in the process. The participants were so moved emotionally they were brought to tears.

This proved to be a phenomenal experience for all. It reminded me of the parent groups I participated in at UCLA: All the participants described the deep pain and joy they felt as they told of their child's attempts to accomplish something. I found the experience so relevant that I knew then that this was the path I should follow.

In addition to loving this learning process, I discovered a most important fact about myself: I not only was eager to learn, but I indeed had a brain! I'd known this, of course. However, I hadn't been able to get past those days when I was young and my family members, although they never stated it, had so few expectations of me, probably because I was a girl. In that era many girls and women were not encouraged to develop their talents as much as the boys and men. Of course, there were exceptions, as witnessed by Supreme Court justices and other lofty positions held by older women today. But those were the exception rather than the rule. Now that I'd proved I was capable of earning a high grade-point in college, I felt the world was open to me, and I could follow my dreams.

## Another "expert"

A week before I graduated in 1979 my mother was diagnosed with uterine cancer. This was quite a shock for our family because my mother was the picture of health and had always been lively and physically strong. My dad had relatively serious heart problems, so, naturally, we thought my mom would outlive my dad. .

We were anxious about Mom, but the doctors had a very positive outlook and reassured us, saying the cancer was small and had not metastasized. They prescribed radiation, followed by a hysterectomy. This treatment was considered routine, and her chances for survival were stated at nearly 100%.

The radiation took six weeks and was tough on her because it was very debilitating. Her surgeon decided to operate earlier than planned because he was leaving on vacation. He reassured all of us that she would be fine. To play it safe, he prescribed massive doses of antibiotics to protect her against any infection she might incur. He also told us that her cancer had shrunk considerably due to the radiation. So with the cancer shrinking, her chances of a full recovery were even greater!

My dad asked the doctor if my mother could wait to have surgery after he returned from his vacation to give her a chance to rest up after her fatiguing ordeal with radiation. "No, I think it wiser if she has her surgery sooner rather than later," the doctor answered. Far be it for us to doubt this expert. (We now know about *experts*!) His reputation was impeccable and unchallengeable, according to our friends' physicians and the physicians in our own family.

My mother had surgery on May 7. She aspirated the night of surgery and developed pneumonia, which spread to both lungs. We were stunned. Overnight, she became critically ill. The doctors were fighting for her life.

Apparently, the massive doses of antibiotics her doctor had prescribed before going on vacation masked the type of infection she'd developed and prevented the attending physicians (more experts!) from finding a correct treatment. No matter how many different things they tried, she continued to lose ground. The physicians stood over her bed gravely watching her struggle while virtually scratching their heads in confusion and despair. She was sliding downhill. It was difficult for us to watch her struggle to live and watch them try so earnestly to save her.

## Standing a vigil

I'll never forget standing a vigil at her bedside with my brother and father watching for any sign of improvement. We couldn't believe what was happening. Soon the rest of our extended family, uncles and aunts and cousins, came to be with us and stayed for hours at the hospital. We were living a nightmare. The doctors were frantically trying to minister to her, but she continued to decline. Every day brought a new problem that baffled her doctors.

We watched her fight for life, and she remained aware and very frightened. Meanwhile, each of the doctors' efforts seemed to exacerbate the problem. They conducted multiple surgeries on her frail body to correct the situation, such as the bleeding ulcers that'd developed along with numerous other complications. She was becoming so irritable that they put her in a medically-induced coma to prevent her body from thrashing, with the idea of getting her out of that state as her body improved. At this point she was no longer aware of anything.

But my mother was dying, and everyone knew it, although the doctors seemed afraid to say as much. My father still held on to the hope that she'd recover. I realized this when he scolded me as I said goodbye to her. He was afraid she would hear me and choose to no longer fight. Yet, I wanted her to feel comfortable letting go because her struggle had been so difficult and painful.

My mother died on May 11, Mother's Day. The brilliant sun that shone through the hospital window spread across her body. It felt so cruel for her to die on such a bright, sunny day. This was five short days after the surgery, surgery that'd been scheduled by the doctor who went on vacation. The copious amounts of antibiotics he'd prescribed had so masked her condition that the attending physicians had been at a loss as to how to correct the situation and save her life. Ironic? Another doctor, another set of attending physicians, another disastrous, unplanned outcome.

On the way to my dad's home, immediately after my mom succumbed, we had to stop at the market for some groceries. He didn't have any food in his house because he'd been staying at the hospital, and we didn't think to ask anyone else to do it. This was a huge effort for us. We went through the motions of picking out food items that I thought he needed, but making such ordinary choices seemed Herculean for my dad and me.

# A great sense of loss

I couldn't help noticing the people around us doing their shopping. It felt surreal. We were moving in slow motion while everyone else seemed to be racing around us. I wanted them all to stop. I felt like screaming at all of them, "How can you be shopping? Don't you see us? Don't any of you know my mother just died?" I felt totally out of touch with my surroundings and filled with a sense of rage. Right then, I realized that everyone at some time in their lives must feel like this when a catastrophe befalls them. I began to think, how many of those people in the market were also feeling their own pain caused by their private losses and misery?

It's not that I hadn't experienced loss before. After all, Dana's placement and death occurred before my mother's passing, and that was tragic, no doubt. Yet, I can't express how miserable I felt for years after my mother's death. It wasn't as though I confided in my mother, or even that we had so much in common. I tried to discover why my grief was so strong, and then I realized that she was truly a mother in every sense of the word. I would miss her unconditional love and acceptance.

Unlike my father, who was more critical, she thought that everything I did was terrific and never failed to let me know that. I grieved deeply that she died so early. She was only 67. If anyone loved life, she did. She was so full of kindness, life and emotion. She had friends that even my father didn't know, proven by the thousands who showed up at her funeral. She touched so many lives, and I loved her deeply. "A girl becomes a woman when her mother dies," it's said. That certainly was true for me. I'd never feel like a girl again.

My dad, although heartbroken, proved to be very courageous following my mother's death. He openly talked about their lives together, and his reminiscences of her seemed to help him heal in what I'd describe as a healthy way. They'd been married for 48 years. Both were loving parents and adoring grandparents. They lived a very full and long life together. He made some good, conscious decisions about how he would mourn my mother. Mostly he stayed close to us, his family, and had little interest in socializing. Finally, after a year, he began to go out with friends.

He was a naturally very active and congenial person, and people had great affection for him. He believed he could never have feelings for another woman in his life, or that his life would ever be the same. He missed my mother terribly. He survived potentially serious surgery two months after my mother's death, which made him realize that he still had some active years remaining.

To everyone's surprise and pleasure, he met a lovely lady and went on to marry her two years later. They were married for four years. We were overjoyed to see him happy and active again, but after several heart attacks and a serious incapacitating stroke, my dad died at 77. Coincidentally, he died the same day that our daughter, Heidi, started college. By the time he died in 1981, which was six years after my mother, I was beginning to work professionally in my chosen field. I felt very sad that he would never see me flourish in this new capacity.

But at least he'd been present at both my college and graduate-school graduations, and I know he was really proud of me. He'd expressed regret that he'd not considered me joining him in his business. I, too, regretted that he hadn't thought of me in that way, but I felt satisfied that I heard those words before he died. What was important was that our relationship grew closer after my mother died.

He adored his grandchildren and had the pleasure of watching them grow and go on to college. For all of those things, I am grateful. Of course, I miss him terribly, but the latter years of his life were sad because he was so ill. It would not be the kind of life he, or anyone else, would have chosen for his remaining days.

Many times, even now, I think about my parents and how much they would enjoy their adorable great-grandchildren. When the grandkids do something special (which is just about always), I feel as though my parents might be looking down on them. Now in my early 70s, I look back with great love and appreciation for my parents. I realize that despite their shortcomings, they were very loving and generous people and left that as a lasting legacy for their children and grandchildren. I hope to leave a similar legacy for my children and grandchildren.

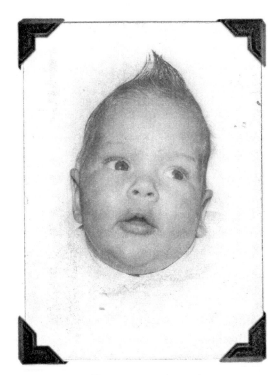

*Dana – 3 months*

*Dana – 6 months*

*Dana – 6 months, Gayle – 21 years*

*Dana – 6 months*

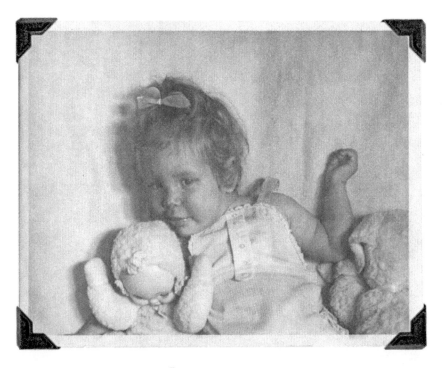

*Dana – 1½ years*

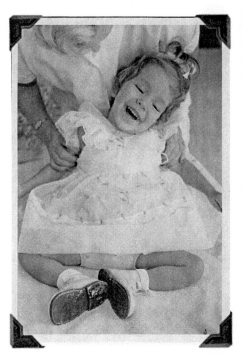

Dana – 2 years

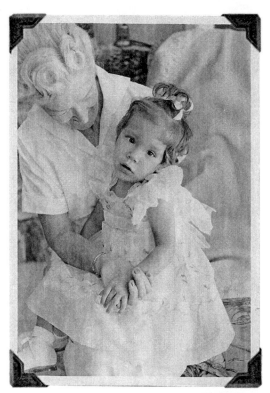

Dana – 2 years

Dana – 2 years
Jebb (cousin) – 3 years
Grandpa

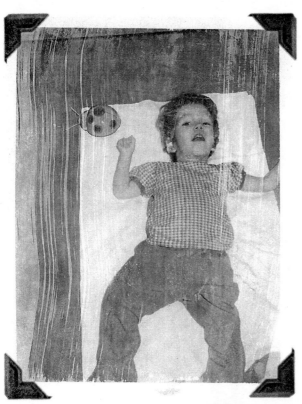

Dana – 3 years

Dana – 4 years

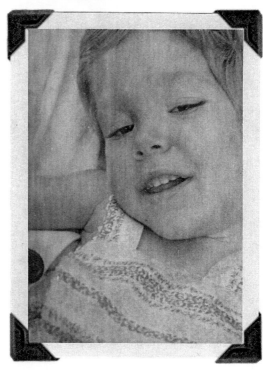

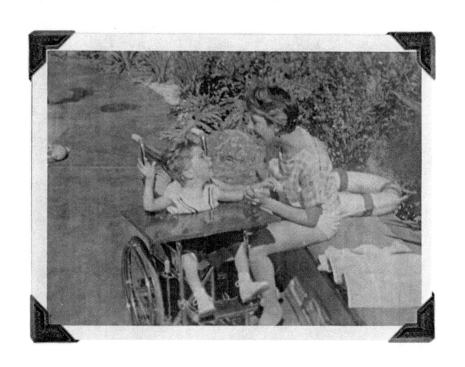

*Dana – 5 years*

*Dana – 7 years*

*Dana – 7 years, with Grandma Freda*

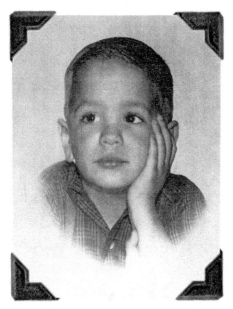

*Left: Scott – 3½ years*
*Below: Heidi – 7 months*

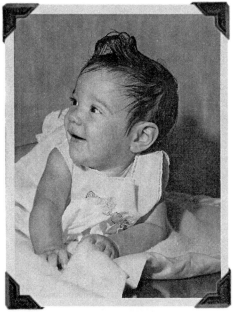

*Gayle & Don*
*1955*

*Left & Above: Don & Gayle*
*Below: Gayle*

129

*Scott – 19 years*
*Heidi – 16 years*

*Scott and Sammy*

*Heidi and Steve*
*Daniel and Matthew*

*Chapter 7*

# Starting a Radically New Program

"Let us put our minds together and see
what life we can make for our children."

—*Sitting Bull*

$I$n 1979, I became excited by an idea and grabbed at the opportunity.

My cousin Marilyn, head of the Parenting Center of the Stephen S. Wise Temple in Los Angeles, urged me to create a program for infants and toddlers with disabilities in which mothers and/or fathers would accompany and participate in the program with their children. Marilyn had been involved with Dana over many years and clearly understood the need for such a program. She felt it was as important for babies and young children with disabilities to have a place to learn and develop.

Although my program would be housed in a Jewish synagogue, it was to be a non-sectarian program with each child's participation underwritten by the California Department of Disabilities. I decided to name it the "Special-Needs Infant/ Toddler Program." (Today, it'd be more appropriately named

"Infant/Toddler Program for Children with Disabilities.") The head rabbi at the temple was thrilled to open up his facility to serve children with disabilities, whatever their faith. What's more, he often dropped by with guests to show off what he considered a jewel of a program.

## A different approach

Our program was one of five early intervention programs in Los Angeles. However, I designed this program to take a different approach than the others. Having been exposed to other programs for many years and having personal knowledge as a mother, I became convinced that we should consider the whole child in relation to his or her environment.

Rather than have physical and speech therapists work only with the child, we decided to use both a professional movement therapist and a speech therapist who would work and play with each child individually, and then together with the parent with the child. The move to include parents as part of our program was strikingly different in those days than any of the other infant programs.

I wanted to include the parents in every aspect of our program. This stemmed from my belief that it was more beneficial for the child to feel as if he or she were playing rather than feeling as if they were showing up to a medical appointment to be corrected or fixed. The goal, of course, was two-fold: enhance the child's development and foster better relationships between parent and child. Many of the interactions were based on modeling behaviors, which the children ultimately grasped over time. We taught the parents how to recognize and model behaviors that would enhance and entice the child's responses.

Our program was creatively crafted into colorful play areas with balls, beanbag chairs, and other motor-activity "tools" the children could use. All our therapists enticed the children by using play and music, which were based in therapeutic interactions.

## Targeting specific needs

The idea was to have the children feel relaxed and have power over their bodies. As they played with their therapists, we were able to watch and identify what each child needed. This was quite different than being assessed by people who focused mostly on the child's disability. That's not to say our program was better than others, but rather that we found different ways to reach the same goals, using creative play and movement. We also tried to help them learn basic fundamental skills, like feeding themselves, washing their hands, combing their hair, the things that are second nature to us all, but not to them. They were very young, but still encouraged to attempt things that were not precluded by their disability.

This made a real difference in the child's responses and learning process. In fact, when the children graduated from our program, many were able to feed themselves with a spoon, an unusual task for children with disabilities at any age. When the program began, I expected it to be immediately successful, but it was difficult getting families to know about us and for children to come and participate. After all, who was I? I wasn't a known expert. Why should I expect to have all the children breaking down doors to attend my innovative program (just because I thought it was great) when there were already four other medically established and proven programs serving infants and toddlers with disabilities?

## *Intense marketing*

It was wonderful to have the confidence and support of my cousin and the temple, but it was another thing to get the children to come to our program. I had expected that everyone would just come. How naïve I was! I was so busy designing the program that I paid little attention how to attract the families and their children. Soon I realized I'd need to do some intense marketing.

One thing I did immediately was to become vendored by the State of California, which gave me accreditation after months of close scrutiny and signing of many papers. That meant I could see children and their families privately at no cost to them and have the state underwrite my services. I realized then that the Stephen S. Wise Temple would have to be vendored as well if its program was to be underwritten. Yet after the temple's vendorization went through, still the children did not come quickly.

I then began trying to educate the regional-center counselors (under the auspices of the Department of Disabilities) about my program. The regional centers, which number five or six across Los Angeles, employ case managers to find suitable programs and services for their clients with disabilities. They serve people from birth to death. These regional centers, which didn't exist when Dana was very young, were formed around the late 1950s or early '60s by parents to help their children receive necessary services. (Leave it to the parents to get things done!)

I planned to personally speak with as many counselors as I could at every regional center that specialized in early childhood to convince them to try our new, inventive program. All the groundwork had been laid. All they had to do was learn about the novel concept, and try it, and then—I was convinced!—they couldn't help but believe in it.

It was quite a task to reach the hundreds of counselors throughout the Los Angeles region. Over several years, I spoke to the various regional-center people both in groups and individually. I visited pediatricians, pediatric neurologists, orthopedists, speech pathologists and physical therapists, audiologists, nutritionists, hospital pediatric social workers, and pre-schools, leaving few roads unexplored. I also reached out to my peer groups, to the other early-intervention programs to let them know about our program.

What was driving me was my passion and fear of failing. I knew my program was innovative. I just had to convince the others that it was right for young children. I banked my heart and soul on this project and its holistic approach because I remembered all too well how separate I felt from the professionals dealing with Dana when she was very young.

I'd had little experience in doing any public relations or advertising, but somehow I knew I was proceeding in the right direction. I was on a mission! I trusted my instincts and followed them. I left my old ways of being insecure and distrust behind me, with a newfound strength and belief that I could make this happen. This was another lesson for me that would be repeated many times over.

# The first client

Lo and behold, someone must have believed in my philosophy, or an angel was watching over me, or both! My first client and her mom were referred to my program through the regional center. I was so excited. That first experience remains imprinted on my mind forever! We were housed in a pleasant little classroom with a mirror across one wall, and some child-sized chairs and tables and baskets filled with toys. Brightly colored mats dotted the floor where the new little girl, Marianna, could lie, and colorful beanbags gave adults a place to sit. Marianna, about age two and a half, was a beautiful child with red hair and blue eyes. She could not yet sit up by herself and had many serious disabilities, including being totally hearing impaired and developmentally delayed. She had a tracheotomy (a tube in her throat) that had to be suctioned regularly by her mother. Her mom was a quiet, lovely woman who was very interested in our philosophy and ready to have her daughter participate in our program.

The mom liked the fact that our interview process was focused as much on the family as on the child. She especially appreciated that we looked at Marianna in a positive light and paid attention to her qualities rather than her deficits. Although we made no promises about Marianna, the mother told us that we made her feel that possibilities existed. I know that, until she came to our program, she felt she was already at the end of the road for Marianna, who was only two and a half! For the first time mom finally felt supported.

The mom told us about her marriage and her preteen daughter from a previous marriage who lived with her and her second husband, Marianna's father. She related to me how difficult

Marianna's disabilities were for her husband because she was his only child and she so strongly resembled him. He was heartbroken about Marianna's condition. Marianna was very headstrong and proved to be a real challenge for her family. (Her case will be described in more detail in a later chapter.) Although the mom appeared in control and calm on the outside, inside she felt very anxious and scared for her daughter. She thirsted to have someone understand her circumstances, and in my program, she felt she'd finally found the haven she was looking for. She, like me in the early years of Dana's life, could find no solace or real understanding from the professionals working with her child.

The mom's friends had dropped away from her, and what family she had didn't understand the depth of her problems. She now felt safe where she could express her anger and guilt over the loss of her "ideal child." She felt sad for her hardworking husband, who longed for a healthy child of his own, and she knew she would never have any more children. I admired both parents for their courage, perseverance, and hard work with their daughter. I learned so much from them and from the many other families with whom I worked during the 15 years at the temple and the 30 years I saw them in private practice. (During that time, I was contact with at least 450 children and their families.) Every moment I spent working with the parents and their children was a time of deep learning and appreciation on my part. I admired the parents' courage and perseverance.

The relationship with Marianna and her family lasted well past Marianna's early childhood, mostly because the mom and dad participated in a parent group that I led. Periodically, they would seek private counseling with me over the years to get through some personal rough spots.

# Marianna's way

With Marianna, life was difficult. For the next three years, as we worked with her, we could see some intelligence peeking through. That gave us hope, yet it was also problematic. She demonstrated her recognition of us and her surroundings by smiling joyfully when she arrived at our program, but at the same time, she was determined and willful little girl, which kept us on our toes. Her willfulness came from her inability to speak or express herself because one could see she was very frustrated in new situations. I felt she was fighting against feeling helpless. Like other children, she felt more secure in knowing what was going to happen next.

She was very rigid and ritualistic in her behavior. Things had to be done her way, and if her rituals were changed she would throw a tantrum and fall apart. When driving to our program, her mother told us, Marianna would insist in clear but unspoken ways that they take the same route; if they didn't, she would get upset. It was amazing how she could communicate her needs.

Her mother was adept in handling her, but that required superhuman strength. From time to time, her mom would tell us that she didn't know if she would make it through the day. We learned from her that we had to be a step ahead of Marianna to help her develop. Her mom had figured out some creative ways to get through to her daughter, which in turn helped us. It took real teamwork to help Marianna grow and develop, but we could never be as masterful as her mother when it came to keeping Marianna out of trouble.

Mom told her regional-center counselor how much she liked our program and the therapist. She especially liked discussion time with me and the other parents, whom she could talk with about her own issues as they related to Marianna. For the first time, she felt supported and less alone. During that period, she could also talk about her concerns about her older daughter and the effect Marianna had on her. In other programs it wasn't common for parents to have time to talk about themselves. But I felt the discussion time was critical so the parents had an outlet to express themselves and feel better about themselves and their parenting skills.

## A pacesetting program

Before long, our reputation grew, bringing in more children and their parents, and the program soon expanded. Originally, the staff was just a therapist and me in that small room. But we added a speech pathologist, a movement therapist, and a volunteer aide, who, incidentally, had mild developmental delay. Besides being helpful, she was terrific with the kids.

We met twice weekly, graduating from the small room to a large, colorful gymnasium equipped with a large mirror and all the apparatus imaginable to assist the therapists in their work with the children. While the therapists were working with the children in a group, I would meet with the parents. We were in the same room, never out of sight, but off to a side and far enough away so the children couldn't hear the conversations or their parents' comments. Thus, we could watch the children while we talked about the parents' concerns and feelings. Parents who wanted to stay with their child could do so for as long they wished. For the most part, the parents relished the time to sit and talk while giving over their control to the therapists or aides working with their child.

Our program was a pacesetter in helping the children become more accustomed to their world around them. Everything we did in the program had a purpose. Our way of working with the children and their parents directly expressed our attitudes of respect for them. By modeling behaviors for both the children and their parents, we could help them develop better interactions between them. The therapists demonstrated techniques to the parents and provided them opportunities to try out some of the communication methods, both in the program and at home.

Attention always was paid to the child's disability, but not at the expense of the child's persona. We emphasized that the disability was part of the child, not the entire child. Often parent and child are so connected that it's difficult for the child to grow and appropriately separate from the parent. This can occur when the parent feels sorry for the child and therefore afraid to challenge their connection.

I remember this was true of me with Dana because she was unable do anything by herself. Before she went into the UCLA program, I was too scared to let go and separate from her. I know that's why I suffered so much when we decided to place her.

## Upbeat and happy

In our approach to the children, we would sit on the floor and crouch low, down to the child's level when near him or her. We did this because we knew that we adults could be viewed as threatening to children because of our size. The last thing we wanted was for them to feel overpowered by us. It wasn't long before we discovered that other programs, after visiting us, began to follow suit. Although we were aware that other programs had borrowed some of the activities from us, we were happy to share.

The mood of the program was upbeat and happy. There was singing with lots of movement. If a child were unable to walk, the therapist would take him/her into her arms and initiate movements that would stimulate them to respond. They participated as best as they could in art projects and outside play in the sandbox and slide. No one would have guessed when entering the room that this was a strict therapeutic program for children with disabilities. When visitors would witness our activities, they would think we were having a great time playing and little more, yet everything was done with a purpose to stimulate and promote the child's development as much as possible. The children never looked as though they were being forced to do anything against their will, and they never seemed unhappy.

We departed from the norm in which therapists typically worked. Our therapists approached the child from where the child was internally at the moment, rather than impose the therapy externally on the child. It was at a relatively slower pace than physical therapy, because the last thing we desired was to impose our theories upon a child, unless the child was ready. Children, generally, are very sensitive to intrusion. The therapist would follow the child's lead by mirroring his or her behavior and respond to the child's cues, encouraging the child to be in control of the relationship. This allowed trust and mutual respect to develop, which hastened the emergence of the child's sense of self to emerge. Then, the child would trust the therapist to do the necessary therapy. The results were amazing to observe.

Group discussions included both the parents' issues and the child's issues, always allowing the parent who needed to talk the first chance to express him/herself. These discussions usually weren't planned, because the parents always had so much on their minds they needed to express. Lively and often emotional, these talks focused on the parents' needs. This naturally reinforced their commonality, making it easier for parents to relate to one another. There was never a loss of words in our groups.

# *A revelation*

One of my favorite exercises came at the end of each day. The parents were asked to sit or lie down on the floor and remain quiet. They were asked to respond to their child non-verbally and to follow their child's lead. The parents quickly saw how much they talked and made unnecessary noise around their children. Many thought that talking to their kids would stimulate their child's speech, but in reality, some of these parents were talking incessantly because they were feeling so anxious, which they realized during the exercise. When they stopped talking and responded silently to their children, they saw their child as never before. For the first time, they saw their child was in charge and able to do things that the parents didn't think was possible.

For example, the child played with Mom or Dad as if he or she were a lovable toy. Or the child would cuddle up closely and rest in the parent's arms, an action the child had never before initiated. The children would show parents their strengths and capabilities by initiating games and finding give-and-take ways to interact. The silent time allowed for the child's increased verbalizations. In fact, on a few occasions, some children uttered their first words. The quieter the parents became, the more in charge the child seemed.

The children and parents enjoyed this activity and were encouraged to do this at home as well. This gave the parents permission to calm down and relax more around their children while paying more attention to what their child was saying or doing. What an amazing revelation!

Snack time was also a very important time for the children. Many turned their noses up when offered food because they had swallowing difficulties or because they weren't usually hungry. So we tried to have snacks that were appealing and easy to eat. Like many toddlers, they may not have been all that interested in eating. But the social situation seemed to increase their curiosity about food. When they were with other children, we could often coax them to eat, but we would never force them if they refused. They had enough problems without us trying to make them eat. However, we did have some surprises. We were successful in teaching some of the children learn to feed themselves with a spoon. The parents couldn't believe that their child who had consistently refused food at home was now independently feeding himself or herself.

## Greater potential

The professionals in our program helped the parents realize their children had greater potential than the parents had believed. The parents often complained that, even when expecting the child to do something minimal, the child would refuse by crying or having tantrums. The therapists explained to the parents that their overprotection and fear prevented the child from advancing, and that all children, no matter how small or severe the disability, can manipulate their parents if the parents allow it.

This was really hard for parents to accept. But the parent's trust of the professionals eventually convinced the parents to elevate their expectations for their children. This required tremendous patience and fortitude on the part of the parents. When they saw their children actually trying and ultimately succeeding at something new, surprises resulted. Everyone was elated!

Of course, this had a direct and positive effect on the parents, giving them the courage to continue to try to diminish their child's manipulation. Parents, even today, fall prey to manipulation without realizing their children are capable of manipulating. Some don't believe their child is able or intelligent enough to manipulate adults. What parents need to understand is that the child is not being manipulative as a means to deceive or hurt the parent but rather to survive. The child learns manipulative devices by responding to either a parent's frantic reactions or non-reactions, or by a parent's overprotection. By making parents aware of what was going on, we helped the parents slowly extricate themselves from this quandary.

## A belated kudo

Eight years had now passed since I left the UCLA program. I was attending a conference where the young UCLA pediatrician who had asked me to leave was the keynote speaker. The infant-toddler program I'd since created was working well. I was sitting in the audience near the front, listening to her speech. In closing, she said, "When I started working at UCLA, I wanted to set the world on fire. I was following in the footsteps of a renowned pediatrician, Dr. Janss. I had my own ideas and goals about working and developing a program, which I thought was all encompassing. However, I met a woman, a mom of a child with a disability, who had attended the UCLA program, years before I arrived. When I came on, she had been working as a volunteer counseling the parents. She felt strongly about the importance of family and its role in caring for their child who had a disability. She emphasized how critical maintaining family mental health is, and how quickly it becomes threatened when there is disability, creating instability and knocking a family off balance.

"As a physician who was new to the UCLA program I was dealing with too many other things to be over-concerned about family issues. That was not my priority. Now eight years later, I have learned from experience that Gayle was correct, that a child does not live in a vacuum, but needs a sound and healthy family to improve and flourish. Gayle Slate is now the director of the Stephen S. Wise Temple Special-Needs Infant-Toddler program where she is successfully proving her theory, by embracing families into her program. I owe her a belated apology and want to congratulate her on being the one to impress upon me to see just how critically important families are in the life of their child with a disability."

With that, she introduced me and asked me to stand. This was so unexpected that I was shocked. I thought that I had died and gone to heaven!

## Chapter 8

# Expanding Our Efforts

"Work is love made visible."
—*Khalil Gibran*

*A*s our program became better known in Los Angeles, a
growing number of callers asked if there was a parent group
in the evenings that both parents could attend. Many of the
moms in our afternoon programs also asked about attending a
parent group for fathers and mothers. They were anxious to have
their spouses participate and share their experiences with other
parents. This was a request I couldn't refuse. It was becoming
clear to the parents in the afternoon discussions that they needed
to understand their whole family system to better cope. As a
result, the children, too, would be better off.

I was so excited to be able to lead this new evening group
because I remembered our own difficulties as well as those of
Margie and Hal. If there'd been a support group for us when we
were young, perhaps I wouldn't have been so anxiety-ridden and
maybe Margie and Hal's marriage would've lasted. Furthermore,
the patterns that were emerging in the afternoon discussions led
us to believe that involving both parents would open up even

more avenues for in-depth discussions and for better possibilities. So I felt I could make a difference for these willing parents.

For the first evening meeting, six couples appeared at the temple's doorstep, eager to begin. Some of the afternoon moms came to the weekly evening sessions with their spouses. We sat on oversized beanbag chairs in a circle in the same gym where we met earlier for the afternoon program. We became acquainted pretty quickly. The parents all expressed a desire to feel better about themselves, their spouses and their children. Many were pretty depressed, and some used their work, liquor or drugs, or anger as an escape.

## Ground rules

I felt a responsibility to interview each family before its members joined the group. That way I could determine the status of the parents' mental health and see if the group was appropriate for them. Neither the group nor the individuals would benefit if among them was a parent with serious emotional problems. In fact, as one parent put it, "You can pretty well compare our home life to being on a roller coaster, and I need to be able to count on other parents who are stable."

In the 30-plus years I've worked with parent groups, I've only come across two parents whose problems were so serious they were unsuited for the group. In those cases, I referred them to outside mental-health specialists.

Before starting the group, I set some ground rules, letting the parents know what behaviors—such as breaching confidentiality, failing to show up, or arriving late—might negatively affect the group. Any of these issues, I explained, could erode trust. In a few cases, parents who didn't abide by the rules had to leave the group, but, mostly, that wasn't a problem.

Unlike the afternoon sessions, which included both parent and child, the evening sessions were for parents only. And as time went on, I learned more about the families from the dads than I'd learned from the moms during the daytime group. The mothers were accustomed to talking about their issues, while the dads initially held back and didn't speak up. But, eventually, they became comfortable talking more about themselves and contributing their viewpoints. In many instances they surprised their wives by accurately describing a situation involving their child that the mothers never knew about.

## Dads' discoveries

One dad discovered his son wanted to be in the kitchen with him, even though Dad knew the kitchen was felt by Mom to be dangerous and should be off limits to the child. One day when Mom was away for a doctor's appointment and Dad was starting to make a sandwich for himself, his son, a poor eater who couldn't talk, motioned to his dad that he wanted to put the sandwich ingredients together. That bonding experience for father and son amazed Mom and thrilled Dad. Although the son never developed into a great eater, the experience began a new trend for Dad and son to find other activities that neither parent would've guessed possible. Dad saw that both he and his wife had been too afraid to allow their son to expand his horizons.

For some, though, the group just wasn't appropriate. Parents who felt uncomfortable in the group were never pressured to contribute or to continue. They could leave, knowing they were always welcome to return. Some parents who left did return later after a crisis or when they felt more ready to join in.

## Painful moments

The group discussions were revealing and eventually helpful for everyone, despite some painful moments. In a relatively short period, I listened to some of the dads reveal that they felt inadequate in their role at home because their wives were generally better at parenting. The men cautiously stated they felt more gratified in the workplace and less successful as fathers. In their minds, they could never be as good in the role of parenting, so why try?

This sometimes created strong negative reactions from their wives, who felt unsupported in caring for their children. The mothers believed they had no choice but to be the primary caretaker for their child because it was hard to keep their husbands involved in the family life. In some cases, fathers wanted little to do with the child, which created hard feelings with their wives. I noticed that the more professional the dads were, the more difficulty they had in accepting their child's disability, especially if a son had the disability. The dads couldn't help feeling that their child somehow reflected them. They suffered disappointment, embarrassment and a sort of shame about their child's condition.

In these instances, insecurity was at the root of the dads' (and sometimes even the moms') feelings of inferiority because they couldn't accept creating an imperfect child. In those cases I was often reminded of a quote by writer Anais Nin: "We don't see things as they are; we see them as we are." How does one who's had real prejudices, unconsciously or consciously, toward people with disabilities suddenly adjust to a disability in their own offspring? How does one bury previous fears and attitudes and begin to see the child within? Many lessons needed to be learned; some of the parents succeeded in learning them, others didn't.

## Control issues

Many times the husbands felt their wives breathing down their necks, telling them how and what to do for their child when the mothers weren't even around. These moms, in truth, were scared to death to leave their husbands in charge, regardless of how able the husbands were in caring for their child. They were fearful that if the dads did anything different, it might have an adverse effect, undoing all the helpful things that'd been done for their child.

Of course, what the wife was really afraid of was letting the dad try out his own methods of caretaking and creativity. Without realizing the damage they were causing, the moms had great anxiety about yielding to their husbands control over what they deemed their territory. This was a no-win situation.

Some parents admitted that they blamed each other for their child's imperfections and took out their feelings on each other. One of the biggest causes of strife was the degree to which they accepted the child's disability. No discussion or solutions could occur if one parent felt nothing was wrong with the child and that the son/daughter would outgrow it while the other parent saw the problem realistically.

One of the dads, a writer, wrote a short treatise about the parent group, called "The Exclusive Club, Our Parent Group." In this paper, he described how he didn't want to be a member and, yet, was thankful for the support of the other parents. The group helped most when the parents could relate to issues and learn to talk honestly and confront what was bothering them. This would result in intense discussions, problem solving, and identifying with each other that made them feel less alone. In many situations, certain problems could not be solved, but by sharing similarities, the problems would be better understood, lessening the tragic feelings and making them more manageable.

Many parents, who'd developed some expertise in certain areas, were able to help others who were just beginning to experience similar situations. For example, when parents were new and coming up against the system (the school, professionals, and the medical community), they felt helpless and inferior. Some of the more experienced parents had been extremely creative in working with the system. Those parents shared their ideas, which helped the newcomers manage and feel less like victims and more efficient in helping their child. The increase in self-esteem was evident as these newer parents learned to become stronger advocates for their children.

## Envy resolved

I'd noticed that initially some of the parents felt envious of other parents because their children appeared less disabled than their own child. These parents wondered how someone who had a child who could walk and talk could possibly feel the same as they. How could they understand what it felt like to have a child who couldn't do *anything*?

But as they listened to the stories, the parents of the more disabled kids grew to know the other parents better and saw they were suffering the same insecurities and anxieties. The degree or type of disability—how the child looked or acted, what the child could or couldn't do—simply didn't matter.

Once this was recognized by all the parents, the similarities became more important than the differences. In fact, some of the children who appeared to be on the cusp of "normalcy" suffered the most. They lacked friends because while they appeared to be only slightly different than the rest of the kids, that difference was keenly felt. Borderline, they weren't accepted by their typical peers or even by adults who didn't quite comprehend their disability. On the other hand, the children in wheelchairs or those with more obvious disabilities often seemed to attract people who wanted to help them. Thus, the public often had higher expectations of the child who appeared less disabled, but who, in fact, was typically less able to fit in.

Getting the parents to recognize their similarities was tough. But all ultimately saw the right of others to be in the group despite the differences in the children's disabilities. Even the single parents who attended were equally involved in sharing. Some parents, however, who couldn't yet tolerate the frankness and open exchanges would leave after a few sessions.

The reason this group worked so well for so many was that the parents respected each other, offering solace and hope while not sugar-coating their responses. A real and honest connection developed. As also happens with people facing ongoing serious illness or other life traumas, the parents initially felt no one else could understand their problems. That created in them feelings of isolation. But once the parents came together, that isolation abated. This comforted them so they felt safe and understood. Although differences existed in the group at times, tremendous growth was visible.

## My own healing

For every moment of growth the parents made, I also grew. Watching and reacting to them made me feel more whole, as if my own healing was taking place. I knew then that Dana's life was not in vain as I was able to witness and help other parents going through parallel experiences.

What I really enjoyed was how they'd reach out to one another outside of our meetings. We had strict rules of confidentiality, and the parents clearly understood they weren't to discuss any members outside the group. However, outside friendships were encouraged, and many in the group became good friends and supported each other.

When problems would arise in the group, it was sometimes because there'd been negative talk or gossip among a few parents outside of our meetings, usually about a particular participant who either talked incessantly or focused too much on himself or herself in the group. Such behind-the-scenes intrigue could threaten to break down trust among the members and even break up the group. I almost always found out about it, and because of the ground rules had been set, this behavior couldn't be ignored. It had to be handled immediately by bringing up the issue in the group discussion, without naming names. By discussing the matter generally, and reminding members of the rules and of the dangers they were creating, everyone was encouraged to preserve camaraderie and safety. However, if the problems continued, then I would have to speak to all the "offenders" privately, which was very delicate to say the least.

## Frustrations

Group discussions often centered on frustrations about professionals who were ineffective or who didn't seem to care—the teacher who wouldn't pay attention to the child in the "included" classroom, the school system that wouldn't provide classroom aides, the regional center case manager who wouldn't assist the parents in getting services, the physician too busy to personally return a call, and many more. Sometimes this would color the parents' feelings about their own child, creating doubt about their hopes and dreams.

For the most, part, these complaints were justified. The parents couldn't understand why so many professionals were unable or unwilling to meet the real needs of the child with disabilities and his/her family. It was intolerable to be rushed out of an office or to not have questions answered sufficiently.

## The IEP process

Of course, exceptions existed. Some professionals were caring and interested. I found myself being asked more and more to serve as an advocate for a child, to sit in at his or her IEP (Individualized Educational Plan) meetings at the schools. These educational plans are required by law to serve all children with disabilities. But seldom did this occur without a battle.

It was difficult for me to sit quietly and listen to some professionals refusing services to the children who were entitled to those services under state law. Everyone in the room knew their excuses were mostly false; the real reason was that services cost money, and money was scarce. The system then—and still is—flawed because of professionals' decisions on whether or how to delegate services. The schools are administratively top heavy, and large amounts are spent on salaries of the paid professionals, which means less can be spent serving children with disabilities. I know the schools have limited money, but the issue is how and where it's chosen to be spent. Commonly, when economic times are tough, services are cut back. But when money eases, seldom are they reinstated.

For years, I sat in sessions listening to parents ask for needed services for their child. But a big obstacle was a revolving-door pattern in IEPs that has existed for years. The professionals (district heads, case managers, teachers, special-education specialists, aides), all of whom are required by law to be present in the IEP to provide services, from time to time would get up and leave the room during the process. Seldom is everyone present at the same time to agree and set the goals for the child's educational program. This blocks the IEP process from continuing, which is against the law.

To hurry the process, the parent is urged by the professionals to sign the documents as soon as possible, even without everyone present. (One parent, a psychiatrist, asked in frustration, "Don't you *want* to help our children improve?")

If the parent won't sign, the IEP is rescheduled over and over again until all the necessary parties are present. Naturally, this creates anger as well as a wearing down of the parents' patience, and precious time is lost in helping the child. This pattern of behavior is costly, prohibitive, and frequent.

If a parent is sophisticated, he or she will take charge and cancel the meeting if everyone involved isn't present or if decisions haven't been agreed upon. But less sophisticated parents may not know their rights and allow themselves to be bullied into signing, just to end the painful process.

Even after the goals are established, the actions to achieve them aren't always carried out, meaning the child doesn't receive the promised services. That puts the school out of compliance with state and federal laws. In many cases, the parents feel so frustrated they feel the need to go to "fair hearings" (a legal term for proceedings overseen by mediators or judges) or go to court to obtain their rights. In many instances, at the last moment just before the hearing, the professional will back down and provide limited services for the child. But most parents don't have the time, the money, or the emotional stamina to seek their rightful services in court.

So, life isn't easy for the parent of a child with a disability. Parents have to cope with the system as it is. They're constantly consumed with worry about the welfare of their child as well as other children in the family. They must fight or give in to the professionals who frustrate them. They must repeatedly take time to regenerate that spent energy. But who has that kind of time?

One of the more savvy mothers was so frustrated by the behavior of a case manager (a teacher) that she confronted him. In her child's IEP, she was asking for 20 speech-therapy sessions for the summer, which the case manager said couldn't be done. Asked why, he said, "Look, I'm breaking my ass for you...don't ask for anything more." Frustrated, the mother stood up (this was her third IEP meeting), and said, "As far as I'm concerned, this meeting is over!" The case manager's action was clearly rude, illegal, and unforgivable. The parent knew he was wrong and that she'd better say something about it rather than be intimidated by his outburst.

She stuck to her guns and eventually won the 20 speech-therapy sessions for her son. But why should she have to go through all of that?

## Times are changing

Something magical seems to happen when children's lives are at stake. Parents suddenly find the courage to speak up and make a difference. Their children have provided them with the incentive to confront inequality. The parents learn to seek support when they need it and stand up to those who oppose them. This includes dealing with family members who aren't supportive and finding those who are. The parent must find that someone important, whether it's a spouse, a sibling, or a friend. They also must earn enough money to be able to survive.

A lot has changed since those early days. Now, many options exist for children who can no longer live at home, and their absence is not treated as finite, as though they've died or disappeared. Of course, it's still a difficult decision for parents to place a child in a setting outside the home. But the time comes, more often than not, for adults with disabilities to live outside the home. It's also more natural for older children to become independent and live away from their families. This is certainly easier than placing a younger child.

Living away from home no longer means that life stops for that person or for his or her family. On the contrary, parents can still be as involved as they wish. They can visit and participate in group-home activities. Children's lives can continue to be enriched. It's not always possible to provide the same stimulation in their family's home as in a group setting. I have seen planned after-school activities and outings that parents can't carry out because of their many other obligations. One can see real caring and attachments develop in the son's or daughter's new life. If the child misses home, they can always go back for visits. After a period of adjustment, parents usually feel relieved that their child has more stimulation.

Once children have fully adjusted to their new home, they usually prefer to stay there with their friends. When older sons or daughters, having become too much of a burden on their aging parents, are placed in a safe and homey environment, they may learn for the first time how to become independent and happier individuals.

Wonderful places have emerged because parents have demanded options for their children. Parents have been instrumental in developing the concept of group homes, and they no longer must feel guilty about "giving up" on their kids. Having these better placements available eases the feelings of guilt and loss that both parent and child have upon separation. The family can continue to be an important part of the child's life, and cost of placement does not have to be a prohibitive factor. (Placement will be discussed further in Chapter 10.)

## Next step in my life

When I first moved to San Diego from Los Angeles, I wasn't sure whether I'd retire, continue practicing, or work in special education. I knew the answer would come to me after I checked out both fields. I understood the special-education field and how to access it because I'd been a major participant and an advocate in special education in Los Angeles. So I decided to network with the special-ed people to see if there was something that I might do professionally in San Diego. As I did in Los Angeles, when I first started my program, I met everyone connected in the special-education field.

I've learned there are no accidents. If one is at all conscious, it's difficult to ignore the signposts that appear in life. One of those signposts was in the form of Mary Shea, the first professional I met in San Diego. She was a very dynamic, bright lady and probably the most important person with whom I could've connected, although I didn't know that at the time. She was an occupational therapist with a master's degree in public health, and she'd just completed a three-year grant as a project director at San Diego State University Foundation. That program, called the Mainstreaming Project, was a "Special Project of Regional and National Significance" (SPRANS grant) and was funded by the National Maternal and Child Health Bureau. As director, Mary developed curriculum to train early childhood educators and family childcare providers to include children with disabilities in natural environments. She trained those providers throughout San Diego County.

We hit it off immediately, and I knew she was a very special and committed lady. Her intention was to return to school for her doctorate as soon as she finished her project, then in its last stage. We met for lunch and must have spent two hours talking about our experiences and philosophies regarding our work with kids with disabilities. She was intelligent, lighthearted, and funny as well as deeply caring. We said goodbye, but I knew we'd see each other again, though I had no idea of the significance of our meeting.

As Don and I settled into our new life in San Diego, Don also explored opportunities to participate in activities. One day he was visited by the executive director of the San Diego Jewish Community Foundation to talk about his joining the board. This organization is responsible for managing personal donor funds, and its board is comprised of volunteers from the community.

At one point during Don's interview, the phone rang. Don had been waiting for an important call, so he excused himself for a few moments. I was in our living room when the JCF executive director, Marjory Kaplan, struck up a casual conversation with me. She inquired about my work and profession. I told her about my interests and work with children with disabilities. Coincidentally, the foundation had just received a generous bequest from Theresa Woodard, a non-Jewish woman who'd had polio all her life. She left the bequest to serve children with disabilities in San Diego County.

The JCF Foundation board was struggling with how and where to donate the money and the most effective way to use the funds. It was thinking of donating some funds to Children's Hospital, some to United Cerebral Palsy, and the rest to various organizations. I suggested this wasn't optimal because the money would dissipate too quickly with too little results. I knew how the money could best be used and told Marjory just how to do it.

## Why segregate at all?

Although my career had centered on disability in early childhood, I'd been in contact with many families with children with disabilities of all ages. Many of these parents complained to me that their kids with disabilities were not being encouraged to attend the same camps and after-school programs alongside other children. Why, they asked, did they need to be segregated at all?

They'd asked me to help them try to change the situation. I sympathized and understood why they needed their kids to be included, but I wasn't then in a position to help. Plus, that would take a great deal of money, which I couldn't begin to figure out how to raise. Further, it'd also take me away from my own program and psychotherapy practice.

When Marjory told me of this marvelous bequest in San Diego, I suggested that if JCF could find a youth organization willing to accommodate children with disabilities into their program, I'd help. Although the Americans with Disabilities Act had been passed five years earlier—making it illegal to discriminate against anyone with disabilities—children with disabilities were for the most part still segregated into disability-specific organizations. Nothing much had changed to help this disabled population. So a perfect opportunity existed to make a real difference in all children's lives.

## *Great enthusiasm*

The JCF board became very excited about the idea and gave its blessings. It sent out a needs-assessment survey to San Diego youth organizations, such as the United Cerebral Palsy, boys and girls clubs and the various YMCAs. The assessments came back with great enthusiasm, offering support and kudos for the idea that children with disabilities should be accepted into after-school programs. Then, we knew, the idea *must* become reality.

One organization that stepped up to the plate immediately was the Lawrence Family Jewish Community Center. Serving the entire community, the center's services are non-sectarian, and it does a great job of including everyone. The young, very able executive director Michael Cohen, who'd grown up at the JCC, and his able associate executive director, Marcia Wolochow, both had always wanted to have children with disabilities participate in their programs. So this program was just waiting to succeed under their tutelage. I suggested none other than Mary Shea to design and operate the inclusion program. She accepted the position, so we were off to a good start.

Don and I, along with Mary and Marjory, helped plan how the money would be divided to cover costs. The funds would be divided into three-year grants, with some money left for unexpected expenses. Before we started, Mary and two other JCC staffers visited a JCC in St. Paul, Minnesota, which was already including children with disabilities. They wanted to see firsthand the model they were using.

I served as chair of an advisory committee that would oversee and monitor the program. Don chaired the long-range planning committee to set up the mission and to establish goals for the program. An attorney and parent of two children with disabilities set up bylaws and before we knew it, we were ready to begin. Everyone on the committee was very enthusiastic and involved in the process. Mary hired a very able, but small, staff to assist her.

Mary was a phenomenon who established a program that was sensitive and inclusive to everyone. Eventually, she trained the entire JCC staff to ensure that the attitudes reflected inclusion in every sense of the word. Their behavior, language, and attitudes, all had to be politically correct. Mostly, everyone accepted the children into their programs with love and deep respect. If the children couldn't participate as actively as some of their friends without disabilities, Mary taught everyone how to accommodate them. If they couldn't play ball, for example, they could be scorekeepers; if they couldn't speak in theatre class, they could operate the lights or curtain. Some games were changed to allow the children with disabilities to participate. Some of the older kids with disabilities even became counselors.

## Mutual benefit

Before long, the community became aware of the JCC's success. And soon typical teenage kids were helping with the program, which made a deep and lasting impression on them.

More and more children were being referred to the program. I couldn't really determine who was more positively affected, the children with *or* without disabilities. For the children with disabilities, their more typical peers were wonderful role models, providing them with a first opportunity to emulate someone and make real friends. On the other hand, the child without disabilities had a first-time opportunity to learn compassion, patience and to see their new friends as people first and kids with disabilities second. And the families of both groups were excited at the opportunity for their children to play together in a safe, non-judgmental atmosphere.

The JCC program was a pilot project. Soon after it began, because of the program's wonderful reputation and quality programming, the National City Boys and Girls Club in a San Diego suburb wanted to take part as well. Because of JCC's success, we knew inclusion had to be made available to more kids across San Diego and, then perhaps, across the United States. But how would we do this? I didn't have a clue, except I knew in my brain and in my heart this was the right thing to do, that inclusion had to be available for those who wanted it.

The idea of inclusion became very appealing to most people once they became familiar with it. Most were surprised that children were still segregated into their own programs. People were excited to donate to the JCC program to keep it viable. But the JCC program was limited by the number of children it could handle, so the time soon arrived to expand inclusion across San Diego.

# Starting KIT

The plan was to continue to fund and support the JCC program for three more years after the Woodard grant money ran out and until the program was financially stable. To continue our JCC support and still create more places for children with disabilities to be accepted, we needed to begin planning right away. In 1997, after two years at the JCC, some of the advisory committee (including my husband Don, Mary Shea, and personal friends) joined me in establishing Kids Included Together (KIT), a non-profit that would provide incentive funding, training, and technical support to youth organizations that would include children with disabilities.

Don and I, along with several members of the JCC inclusion-advisory committee, formed a strategic-planning board, which, after six weeks of intensive planning, would evolve into the first KIT board. After coming up with a creative plan, KIT was born.

Although organizations expressed interest in including the children, we thought we still had to entice them not only with technical support but also with a small financial incentive. The first year KIT awarded grants to several organizations including a boys and girls club, a children's dance organization, a YMCA and a local parks and recreation department. Setting up this large non-profit was a gargantuan task because this would be the first organization of its kind in the United States. I was in charge, but I'd never created anything like this. We weren't quite sure whether, for example, we should be hands-on, or just send in our professionals, or only provide training. Also unclear was if we'd continue funding to a few large organizations or spread inclusion to a larger number of small ones.

## Magic happens

It was ambitious to expect organizations to break from their usual ways of operating to include children with disabilities. It took several months to convince some groups to come on board. But once they saw the JCC and other youth-development programs accepting the children, they gained the confidence to try inclusion. What they didn't realize at first is that it's against the law to discriminate against anyone, and children with disabilities can't be refused services. The law is more than symbolic. It was meant to break down the barriers, and KIT was prepared to help organizations eliminate these barriers anyway it could. We were ready to make inclusion stick because society needed to see value in all people, regardless of disability.

We were constantly being tested, moving forward and backward a few steps. However, magic began to happen as we established our board and things began to fall into place. I became the executive director/president of the board and asked some personal friends to join me on the board. Mary Shea and several JCC executives were extremely helpful in planning for KIT.

I don't think a day went by that I didn't speak to Mary. She was a powerhouse who energized me. She was a tremendous support who knew just what to do. I was in my late 50s at the time, and like Mary, I had much energy and passion. I was excited about the prospect that children with disabilities would never be discriminated against as Dana had been when she was young. I knew this was an opportunity to make an important change.

# Much to do

Yet, there was so much to do. At night, thoughts of KIT and things to do invaded my quiet space. Ideas kept roaring through my head as I sought to sleep. I finally learned to keep a notepad near my bed to jot down overflowing thoughts. Once they were committed to paper, rest would finally come.

Now it was time to make it happen. First, we had to provide grant funding to the first five programs. As the JCC had done, we agreed to fund them for three years if they met minimum reporting requirements. The first recipients, and particularly the Boys and Girls Club, were phenomenal because they were excited and willing participants, eager to begin. We, in turn, had to raise funds, which was not easy then, as it is not easy now.

One of the new board members established a women's support group to hold galas and teas. Several board members, along with Mary and me, began to visit various organizations to let them know about KIT. I personally visited at least 50 organizations as well as encouraging the Department of Disabilities (Regional Center) to refer their disabled clients to our programs. Mary Shea, who'd become a KIT employee, wrote several continuous grants to the San Diego Regional Center, and the center was so impressed with the mission that it funded KIT for four years.

We found that partnerships like the JCC, the Boys and Girls Clubs, and the Regional Center were the cornerstones of our success. This was because San Diego at that time was a collaborative place that brought people together. The Boys and Girls Club was an immediate success because it provided a natural setting for after-school programs. Working parents could leave their children during the summer from 6 a.m. until

6 p.m., knowing their children would be safe and well-cared for. Now brothers and sisters for the first time were able to attend together instead of parents taking their child with the disability to a different, special after-school program.

The Boys and Girls Club of National City hired an inclusion director, a man who happened to have disabilities. He was an inspiration to all the kids. Before very long, they forgot about his and everyone else's disabilities and focused on how much fun they were having together. Both organizations, the JCC and the Boys and Girls Club of National City, succeeded in their efforts because everyone in their facility and on their boards so willingly embraced the concept.

Before very long, other organizations became part of the KIT family. Several YMCAs, parks and recreation programs, dance and theater arts programs, like the Carlsbad Boys and Girls Club came onboard. All were exceptional in their willingness to accept children with disabilities. Jan Giacinti, executive director of the Carlsbad Boys and Girls Club, was so excited about inclusion that she later joined KIT; she's now the current and passionately driven CEO. Previously, Mary Shea had served as KIT's official executive director for the first three years, a very formative time. Mary stepped down from the post to become KIT's director of site development, a key position, for several years and now serves as a regular consultant to KIT.

## *Big results*

KIT has become what I'd hoped: a renowned non-profit organization specializing in providing best-practices training for community-based youth organizations committed to including children with disabilities into their existing recreational, social, and child-care programs. It focuses on sustainability so organizations will continue to provide inclusive environments long after KIT's involvement has ceased.

In the early days at the JCC and at the National City Boys and Girls Club, KIT served perhaps 50 children at the most. Now, more than 10 years later, it includes 46 affiliate organizations with 199 sites in San Diego County, and is growing daily by leaps and bounds. In the most recent fiscal year, KIT trained 2,872 youth providers in the best practices in inclusions.

Since its founding in 1997, more than 5,800 children with disabilities have been co-enrolled with more than 82,000 typically developing youth at KIT affiliate sites. This translates to 399,470 hours of inclusive youth programs.

## New strategies

Our goals and strategies have evolved. For one thing, we found that by funding "inclusion programs" within the organizations, we weren't helping children feel the same as everyone else. Rather, the kids within the inclusion program were still being seen as separate. When people referred to the kids with disabilities, they were seen as "those kids" in that inclusion program.

Mary astutely suggested doing away with the words and concept of an "inclusion program" and instead bring the idea of inclusion under the auspices of the entire organization. Instead of hiring and training an inclusion director, KIT began to train the recreational directors and all of the organization's employees so that inclusion would become all-encompassing within the entire organization. In that way, all people, not just children with disabilities, would be welcomed as equals into their organizations and participate like everyone else. The word "program" would be dropped, thereby eliminating the sense of separateness and fragmentation. This reminds me of my early infant-toddler program when I felt it was crucial to see the child as part of the whole rather than a separate entity.

Secondly, we also changed our way of funding. Sure, organizations need some funds to begin. But we noticed that the larger groups didn't use as much as they thought they needed to begin the process. They also bought into the idea of inclusion and came to feel, as I'd hoped they would, that they didn't need to be paid to do this.

Thirdly, we also began to realize that our best efforts would be to provide aides and more training to spread inclusion more quickly to more organizations. This turned out to be what worked best.

So rather than donating larger amounts to big organizations, we restructured KIT as a training and technical-support program, which allowed us to reach out to more organizations. Many groups began to call us to ask us about specific problems regarding children with disabilities in their programs. And now KIT's training is so much in demand that we've established licensing agreements with organizations that have undergone KIT training and have qualified as KIT-certified inclusive organizations.

In 2006, KIT's National Training Institute on Inclusion was recognized as an official "go-to" organization, which signals a certain maturity. In fact, KIT is the only organization of its kind in the United States to be so designated. This occurred because of the knowledge and professionalism of the KIT staff, KIT's superior board members, and kudos from those whom KIT has served. Since my tenure as president and chairman of the board, the successive KIT presidents all have taken KIT to new levels, far beyond my expectations. KIT has expanded throughout and beyond San Diego. The talented and dedicated KIT staff, many who still remain from KIT's inception in 1997, serve as the organization's backbone. They are the true "dream team," although there are only five fulltime and three part-time employees to do a huge job.

## *Our mission expands*

Along with the current 46 San Diego organizations, a KIT chapter has been formed in Los Angeles where, for example, we have served "L.A's Best," a youth organization serving over 100,000 children with and without disabilities, and the Santa Monica Boys and Girls Club. In addition, the Lanterman Regional Center is closely involved with KIT LA, offering support and referrals to many organizations. Next, we'll be looking toward San Francisco with the same mission of assisting youth organizations to include children with disabilities. We hosted our first national conference in 2004, and our fourth in the spring of 2008. Our goal of being accepted nationally is being met as people from all over the United States attend our conferences to bring inclusion into their organizations.

KIT regularly receives calls from across the country, asking that KIT be brought to their cities. The more the better! KIT has moved into its new, permanent home—known as the National

Training Center on Inclusion—in the Point Loma neighborhood of San Diego. It's a state-of-the-art facility and learning lab that creates and disseminates best-practice information. NTCI offers live training, eLearning and a library of books, videos/DVDs, and other material related to inclusion and disability for use by youth providers and KIT trainers.

Our mission is succeeding and exploding right in front of our faces! We've trained organizations from over 22 states and continue receiving calls from across the country. You see, it was the *right* thing to do!

## *Feedback*

KIT has generated tremendous interest and support from organizations that support children with or without disabilities. In fact, it's been awarded several major grants from non-profits as well as government agencies. But to me, even more telling are the many testimonials we receive.

Here's just a small sampling:

- "Inclusion has helped our children look past the disabilities and see the person inside."

- "A program like KIT teaches tolerance and respect, for all people, whatever their differences. In the case of kids with disabilities, they're not all that different; they just need a little help."

- "Inclusion means that we treat all kids the same. We're going to make whatever accommodations we need for specific kids, but basically we're trying to get them all to be the best kids they can be."

- "We have seen children and parents look past the disabilities and embrace a philosophy where everyone can participate in any program, class, activity, day camp, or swim class."

- "Inclusion helps children discover their hidden talents and to bring out their individual strengths and abilities."

## Looking back

I am humbled beyond words how the KIT people have taken the steps to advance the organization to such a high level of accomplishment. I can't forget the monumental challenges facing me during KIT's early beginnings. Because I'd never operated a business or been in charge of a large operation, KIT took over my life. I constantly worried about it not succeeding. I struggled as if I were Sisyphus pushing a huge boulder up the mountain. I couldn't let go out of fear the boulder would fall back, and crumble and destroy me. Until that boulder reached the top to stay, I dared not let go. As people joined me in that struggle, my confidence grew. I felt buoyed by their support, although there were many fits and starts during that period.

But I got to the place when I knew I could no longer carry the burden alone. I asked Mary Shea to step up and become the first official executive director. Previously, I'd had the help of a part-time professional grant writer whom I solely depended upon for raising money through grants. Until Mary stepped up, we didn't have the money to spend on other professionals. Before Mary became executive director, I depended on our treasurer to help us find ways to be frugal and creative with the money that we raised. Somehow, with her help and Don's input, we made KIT live!

Don's support of me from the very beginning kept me afloat. Not only did he encourage me to go to college and obtain my graduate degree, he joined my journey and walked every inch of the way to found KIT. He felt proud that he could partner with me to help so many families and their children with disabilities finally become accepted in society as equals.

He and I spent hours and hours talking, consumed with KIT's trials and errors. Now we can finally enjoy the fruits of KIT's hard work and success. I still periodically fight off my old fears of failure until I look at what the people at KIT are actually accomplishing. These wonderfully committed and hardworking individuals make it work. I could've never accomplished as much as I have if Don wasn't in my corner. Now, to add a beautiful note to this testimony, the next generation—our daughter Heidi—has worked diligently as a member of the KIT board.

For many years, both Scott and Heidi have continued to be great financial supporters of KIT, but Heidi has actively worked hard to keep KIT growing. Despite being busy with her two young sons, Heidi volunteered countless hours to put on KIT's Holiday Teas, which have been highly successful in raising friends as well as funds. In addition to the Holiday Teas, she served on the board as the secretary and member of program committee, one of the key committees that carry out the mission of KIT. Dana has truly left a legacy that will go on to serve thousands more!

## Chapter 9

# Looking at Families from the Inside Out

"There are as many ways to live and grow as there are people. Our own ways are the only ways that should matter to us."

*—-Evelyn Mandel*

*E*very family is unique. And families who have a child with a disability are no different. They're composed of ordinary people—not superheroes—who deal with their experiences as best as they can. In so doing, they often discover an amazing strength and character they didn't know they had.

So far in this book I've written a lot about families in general terms, but getting more specific and talking about individual families may help you better understand what family members go through when they have a child with disabilities. The stories that follow are personal and true, though I've taken the liberty of changing names.

That random and sometimes unfortunate events that happen is difficult for us to accept. Because we have no control over such events, they underscore our vulnerability. Why do such random things happen? It's not because people are selected based on their strengths, intelligence, wealth, or ability to cope. Nor are they being punished by a vengeful God for something they may have done wrong, although some have made more than their share of poor decisions.

Instead, it just *happened*. And as you'll see, what happens is, in the final analysis, less important than how we react and adapt.

## Caroline, Christy, and the Dream

I met Christy when she was in her late 20s. She was in a difficult marriage with a Frenchman, a chef who had difficulty keeping jobs due to a serious drinking problem. Christy came to see me because her two-year-old daughter Caroline had suffered anoxia (lack of oxygen) at birth that left her with CP. Caroline was an adorable little, blonde with pretty blue eyes. Her mother was very proud of her but terribly worried about her disability. She said that she'd dreamed that if she had a girl, the daughter would have a wonderful wedding and wear the most beautiful wedding dress.

Now that she had a daughter, that dream kept haunting and eluding Christy as she discovered more and more about Caroline's disability. From the very beginning, her husband showed relatively little interest and concern for his child. He never wanted anything to do with people with disabilities because of earlier experiences with members of his family who had disabilities. This, of course, left Christy alone to deal with all the problems that came up for her daughter.

Arguments began to build between Christy and her husband, who began to drink even more heavily, and that led to a bitter divorce. In addition to the enmity between them, Christy asked in vain for years for her ex to give Caroline her deserved child support. Aside from continuously and unsuccessfully bringing her ex into court for back child support, Christy anguished over not having enough money to care for Caroline.

Christy had no one to talk to other than her mother, who was supportive, and her few friends, who didn't really understand the seriousness of her situation. In addition to worrying about how she was going to survive, she was most anxious about her daughter's progress. Christy's anxiety was building into serious panic attacks, especially the day she brought Caroline to my office. It was there that Caroline experienced her first seizure, which scared us both, but especially her mother.

She called the paramedics from my office. Caroline recovered quickly without harm, but Christy was shaken, agonizing over the possibility that her daughter was going to be epileptic in addition to having CP—just one more problem to add to her already difficult situation. The seizures gradually subsided over time with medication, and Christy's worst fears were not realized. But as their lives progressed, they encountered many ordeals caused by Caroline's CP. Both mother and daughter struggled to overcome Caroline's physical problems.

As she grew older, Caroline tried in great earnest to capture her unapproachable father's love and attention, but she was met with disinterest and broken promises. She was overjoyed, for instance, when she heard that his new wife was going to have a baby. Caroline could hardly wait to welcome her new baby brother for whom she planned to baby-sit and care for like the big sister she had envisioned herself.

Her father and stepmother had other ideas, however. Neither of them had any plans to include Caroline in their lives. When Caroline called and asked to come over to see the baby, they refused. This was so shocking and tough on Caroline that she took out her anger on her mother, adding more stress to their already difficult situation. Christy was doing everything she could to help her daughter improve and have a reasonably good life. She sacrificed greatly to ensure that Caroline could receive the needed therapies and equipment. She balanced her life between her full time jobs and Caroline's needs.

One can imagine Christy's feelings of hurt, anger and disappointment when her daughter was unloving and nasty to her, while Caroline was longing for her father's love and attention. Life was not treating Christy or Caroline fairly. By this time, Caroline was not quite a teenager, and her physical condition was quickly deteriorating. She increasingly struggled to walk as her upper torso lost strength. Christy feared her daughter would lose ground and stop walking altogether.

An attractive woman, Christy had occasional serious relationships with men, but nothing came of them. She constantly worried that having a child with a disability might send her suitors away. She was beginning to believe that love was not in the picture for her.

As Christy wended her way through the world of special education and disability, she became very adept in securing services for her daughter. She was clever and resourceful and seldom accepted no as an answer from professionals. She became a real advocate and role model for her daughter. Along the way, she and her daughter experienced many disappointments and frustrations, but the small successes were huge. In the parent group, she described her feelings as "going into a tunnel and coming out into the sunlight."

Although her worst fear—of Caroline ending up in a wheelchair—did come true, Christy found that reality didn't destroy her or her daughter. Not only did they both become stronger, but Caroline went into therapy to work on accepting the truth that her father was never going to be in her life. This has been one of Caroline's biggest challenges, but she has become accustomed to not having everything she most desires. It's sad, but true.

Caroline turned 18 and was provided with a van as well as an aide to drive her and help her manage. She attends college and has trained a special dog to assist her. Christy has worked very hard to help her daughter become as independent as possible. She's been Caroline's strength through surgeries and emotional challenges, which Caroline clearly understands. Christy doesn't feel sorry for Caroline, and this is shown by the very clear boundaries she has set for her daughter. Christy's perseverance and strong will has gotten them both through very difficult times and allowed them to overcome most of the obstacles between them.

Christy bought a home, and then fell in love with a man whom she married and brought into her home. Her daughter "stood up" for her at the wedding and warmly welcomed her stepfather and stepbrother into their lives. Life was beginning to improve for the two women. For a while Caroline was happy for her mom while she herself began to enjoy real independence.

Christy left Caroline alone at home (at Caroline's insistence) for a week last summer. Caroline mastered the situation and took complete care of herself, making her mother and herself very proud. Caroline's special dog assists her, and Caroline is solely responsible for the animal's care. Due to her newfound success in handling her responsibilities, Caroline will soon be moving into her own home with roommates while she continues her college education.

If you're wondering how this all came about, chalk it up to Christy's tenacity and perseverance. She won her day in court, forcing her ex-husband to finally come up with $60,000 in back child support. That and hard work allowed Christy to purchase her new home, a van for Caroline, and eventually a new home for Caroline, too. Sadly, Christy's marriage is faltering, but knowing her as I do, I'm sure she'll face her challenges yet again with courage and aplomb.

I first became acquainted with Christy in the Los Angeles parent group, where she participated for 10 years. As luck would have it, she moved to San Diego at the same time as I, in 1993 and took it upon herself to start a group for moms of children with disabilities, which has been ongoing. I've been witness to Caroline and Christy's growth and feel so fortunate to have played a minor role in the lives of these two very special people.

## Revisiting Marianna

As Marianna (discussed in Chapter 7) grew, life didn't become easier for her or for her family. In addition to a tracheal tube inserted to help her breathe, she'd had since birth a tube inserted into her stomach to provide liquid nourishment. But that wasn't sufficient for her to continue growing. Because she'd never swallowed food, she also never learned to use her teeth or muscles in her tongue, mouth, or throat.

Her mother and father, along with her doctors, felt it was time for the tube to come out because she needed to learn to eat regular food in order to thrive. For Marianna, having never eaten a morsel of food, learning to do this was a very daunting task. It'd mean removing both the gastric tube from her stomach and the tracheal tube from her throat. The doctors felt she'd be able to breathe on her own and learn to eat, despite the challenges involved, and it'd no longer be necessary for her mother to drain her trachea.

No one quite knew what the next step was to be. How does a child with mental challenges suddenly learn to do something that has been so foreign to her? The task would be a life-and-death issue. Both parents, after much deliberation and with great trepidation, planned to take a week to try to get Marianna to eat food.

They didn't know what to expect, although they knew for sure that Marianna would resist and fight every inch of the way, which was her typical response to new experiences. Her parents, unsure if their plan would work, agreed to take off work and stand firm against Marianna's will. They remembered how she repeatedly crawled out of her crib and walked out the door into the street. And they remembered the great trouble bringing her back home and putting her back into her bed. In fact, she was so determined to continue leaving the house that her parents had to erect a kind of cage to keep her imprisoned in bed.

Life with Marianna brought many such grim frustrations because she fought her parents continuously. Her deafness and disabilities prevented her from understanding their intentions. Therefore, their actions made no sense to her. Whatever they did to protect her was interpreted by Marianna as punishment.

To get her to begin to eat, the parents had to first teach her how to put food in her mouth. She refused, by turning her head violently from side to side, not allowing them to get near her mouth. After several days, they had to resort to pinning her down and climbing on top of her to get her to swallow a teaspoon of applesauce, which she promptly spit out at them.

She clawed at them, crying and running away from them and wearing down both herself and them. Still, she wouldn't eat a morsel. This ordeal went on for days in her bedroom, where most of the furniture had been removed; the rest of the house was closed off to her. She barely slept, and neither did her parents. This misery went on for more than a week with her taking in only water through a straw. They were exhausted and soaking wet at the end of each day. Even though her parents felt as if they were being cruel (and feared hurting her), they knew they must get her to eat or she wouldn't survive. They also knew that their daughter would react exactly in this way.

Although she ran in circles around her room to keep her parents away, she finally gave in and ate some baby food. That was a huge success for her, even though she didn't comprehend the concept.

Marianna was not an affectionate child. Although her parents wanted to hold her close and soothe her, affection was a tremendously difficult concept for her to accept. So she didn't understand they were trying to get her to eat because they loved her. She felt their determination was hostile. What child wouldn't?

Even today, after knowing so many brave parents, I've never witnessed such courage as I did in these parents. Every move they made to save their child was felt by her to be barbaric and unrelenting, yet they did all they could to save her from dying. And they succeeded.

After attending her public school's special classes, Marianna later went on to live at a school in the desert for hearing-impaired children. She finally learned to eat, and become better behaved, though her disabilities were too involved to have her live at home. She now lives in a group home with other young adults with disabilities. Her parents are doing well, and both are working in their chosen fields, something that was thought to be impossible at one time.

## Chloe Fears the Truth

One day, Chloe, mother of a young boy with CP and other undiagnosed conditions, heard her son's teacher apply a diagnosis of Asperger's Syndrome to her son. (Asperger's is a type of Autism with high intellectual functioning.) The mother, after hearing the teacher's opinion, was shocked and devastated, despite the fact that she knew her son's flapping arm movements and repetitive behaviors were typical of Autism. Awestruck over her son's brilliance and thought processes, Chloe was angry with the teacher for diagnosing him.

She asked, "How could he have Asperger's and be so bright?" Later, when she recognized the real possibility that he did have Asperger's, she told the mothers in our group she didn't understand why she'd been so upset when she herself clearly saw his odd behaviors for quite a while. She'd known on some level that he could have autism, but the realization was too painful for her to accept.

That's a common reaction. As long as the secret remains hidden, parents can sometimes fool themselves by trying to control their situation and dealing with it the best way they know how. Even though they realize the truth on some level, it's shocking to hear it spoken. Doubts begin to rise as they worry if they have what it takes to help their child, or even handle the truth emotionally.

In Chloe's case, once doctors confirmed the teacher's opinion, her fears were realized. She had prayed that the teacher was wrong. So the official diagnosis threw her into depression and despair all over again, just as when she first discovered that her son had CP. Now there were two diagnoses. How could she manage this second blow?

When the real diagnosis is made, a parent's fantasized ideal is shot down. This causes the parents to feel even more out of control and helpless. They feel like failures. No matter how much they've done to help their child, it seems as if that wasn't enough. Ultimately, though with difficulty, they come to accept the truth about their child. Once that happens, they can deal with their child as he or she really is.

Actually, Chloe's son made better progress than the mother could ever have imagined. As with many people with Asperger's Syndrome, he was quite gifted and creative. Chloe discovered her inner strength, dedicating time and energy to looking into a treatment recommended for children with Autism/Asperger's Syndrome. She decided to take a risk and get the recommended treatment for him, even though that would involve most of the summer and require her to stay with him daily for hours at a time inside a hyperbaric chamber. Doing so would also require her husband and her 14-year-old daughter to manage without her, which was difficult especially during summertime.

However, both mother and son personally realized very positive results from the experience. Chloe, who had suffered bouts of depression, felt much improved, and her son became calmer and more focused. His temper tantrums subsided, and he became happier. The rigid behaviors and hand flapping also subsided. He was now able to enter regular kindergarten where he was able to tolerate learning and participate in a classroom with children without disabilities.

For the first time Chloe began to feel more hopeful about the future for her son and for her family as well. She also began to realize that she could survive almost anything and thus came through this very difficult period with newfound confidence.

## Jeanine and Gary, a Couple with Good Genes

Jeanine and Gary came to see me privately when they discovered their son Adam had Down Syndrome, a chromosomal abnormality. At the beginning, while in the hospital, Jeanine didn't want to see her son after she heard the diagnosis. "It wasn't supposed to be this way," she said, angry, distraught and terribly disappointed. Once they were home, she had difficulty bonding with Adam. Gary was so worried that their son was not going to thrive because of Jeanine's avoidance of him that he suggested both he and Jeanine come to see me.

They brought Adam with them, and when I saw him, I couldn't believe how beautiful he was: a red-headed, blue-eyed, chubby baby who captured my heart. The mom was surprised by my reaction. It was not what she'd expected. I think she really didn't believe me or thought I was just trying to make her feel better. She obviously couldn't get past the diagnosis of Down Syndrome to appreciate her son's obvious gifts. Her husband bonded with his son and seemed to accept the reality far more readily than his wife did.

As time passed, though, Jeanine's feelings began to change. It wasn't long before her loving feelings toward her son took over, leaving behind her catastrophic disappointment. As she cared for him, Adam's disability stopped looming larger than Adam.

She and her husband had lived together for many years before their son was born. Initially, they'd never planned to have children at all. When they changed their mind, it was largely because they felt they had a good gene pool and their child would be smart and accomplished. When they discovered their son had a lifetime disability, the shock initially was too much for Jeanine. But as she changed, she began to accept Adam and make plans for him. Jeanine turned into a devoted mom to her adorable son.

At one year old, Adam joined my early-childhood program where he did quite well. He was so lovable and funny that none of us could resist his charm. Jeanine said, "We really don't belong here. Adam is so much better than the other kids."

I thought to myself, "We'll see."

He seemed to be doing fine in the program until one afternoon his body started to thrust forward violently as he was playing. Jeanine didn't know quite what it was, but I recognized it as a seizure. It was all too familiar to me, yet a surprise because the boy hadn't been ill, nor did he have a fever, which is usually the forerunner of seizures. It was also not typical for a child with Down Syndrome.

Jeanine took Adam to her pediatrician and to a pediatric neurologist. Adam was diagnosed with West Syndrome, a rare form of infantile epilepsy. Once again, Jeanine fell into a depression, but not quite as debilitating as the one she'd experienced at Adam's birth. She now had professionals to help her, and she found new doctors she could depend on to find medication to control Adam's seizures. Support was there as it hadn't been when she first discovered Adam's disability. Finding the right medication was critical because these seizures could deter any developmental progress that Adam had been making.

Both parents were upset, but now Gary, the dad, fell apart and started drinking heavily. This had been an earlier problem in his life, and alcohol became his drug of choice to help through his pain. Gary felt this second diagnosis to be so unfair, and that thought plagued him through the years as Adam was growing up. Adding to Gary's angst was he didn't feel particularly satisfied with his job as a high school coach.

Then came the final blow: Adam received a third diagnosis, autism. How could this be? How could their perfect son have not one, but three terrible diagnoses? Gary railed against the unfairness of it all as he struggled through therapy and tried to stop drinking. As a result of a DUI (driving under the influence) arrest, he went into a rehab program for a month to stop drinking, which worked for a while.

Although he loved his child and his wife, he felt morose all the time. He'd come to see me in therapy where it became clear his morbidity was the overriding topic. Gary's approach to life was negative and hopeless as evidenced by his bleak outlook. Much later, he was diagnosed with bipolar disease (also known as Manic Depression.)

Jeanine, on the other hand, became stronger, and although sad, she accepted the reality that her son was never going to accomplish very much. She often spoke of how picturing Adam as a severely disabled adult "blew her away." But, fortunately, she was able to work everyday with Adam and generally enjoy her family despite her fears and Gary's problems. She learned to appreciate Adam's qualities, and with the help of the group and professionals in my program, she became more equipped to handle life in general.

Then, a few years later, she discovered she was pregnant. Of course, both parents were very nervous, but hopeful about having another chance of having a typically developing child. When their second son, Soren was born, they were ecstatic. However, around two years old, Soren began displaying certain familiar behaviors that troubled Jeanine. Frightened, she rushed him to the specialist who'd diagnosed his older brother Adam.

The diagnosis again was Autism, which Jeanine had guessed before ever seeing the doctor. Soren was diagnosed with Asperger's Syndrome, a higher-functioning form of Autism. She was devastated once again and wondered if she somehow had made God angry with her.

This seemed too much for her to handle, but handle it she did. Like so many parents of children with disabilities, Jeanine rose to the occasion. By this time she'd discovered she was a survivor. She loved her children deeply and out of that love, she managed her responsibilities and busy life without missing a beat. Gary had a tougher time with depression. Although he was a good father to his sons, he had a more difficult time than his wife and, from time to time, chose to go off his medication for the bipolar condition. Ultimately, he preferred not to take any medication, which caused him to increasingly suffer melancholia.

After I moved to San Diego in 1991, I asked Jeanine and Gary to serve on a parent panel of a seminar I designed at the University of California at San Diego. (Titled "Building the Relationship between Professionals and Parents of Children with Disabilities," it involved role-playing in which each group assumed the other's role and in so doing learned firsthand of the other's plight. Of course, as expected, the professionals learned much more about the parental experience than the parents learned about the professionals.) Jeanine and Gary had become able advocates in seeking services for their children and were well-versed in the system. They were helpful in the seminar to both the professionals and parents by clarifying the issues between them. It was an experience that placed them for a change on the giving side rather on the receiving side.

It'd been 12 years since I'd last seen them, and needing to hear about the status of their family and their sons, I called them not long ago. I spoke to Jeanine, and she filled me in. Her son, Adam, now 24, has entered a residential group home and is once again having seizures and medical problems. Soren, almost 20, is doing well in academics, but has few friends, a common experience for kids with disabilities. He's smart enough to know that he is different, which causes him deep depression.

In speaking to Jeanine, I found her to be thoughtful and accepting, but sad. Now when she speaks of her sons, she occasionally uses soft humor to balance the pain she's felt throughout these years. She surprised me by saying that she thought that her dad, who recently died, and perhaps her brother, also had Asperger's Syndrome, which I thought was ironic because of the earlier reference to the good gene pool. It's a miracle how this family gets through a day, but it does so with hope, courage, a sense of humor and acceptance.

## Paul, a Dad's Guilt

Paul and Diane had a son Robert, a very young child with severe disabilities. Robert had been in the hospital where he almost died so many times that his parents lost count. Their lives were centered on Robert, and they were extremely depressed when they joined the Los Angeles parent group. They never knew when their child would fall ill, so they lived on a tightrope waiting for the next illness to take him. Robert was unable to sit or stand and appeared much younger than his age. He could do very little on his own and was completely dependent upon his parents.

Their marriage was suffering terribly and when I met them. Both parents had extremely sad expressions. They hardly ever left Robert, which only increased their feelings of isolation and depression. They earnestly believed their son would improve and that, with enough therapy, he would ultimately stand and walk. They wouldn't give up on him and counted upon his improving. But that was not to happen.

The parent group helped them because it was the first place they felt as though they belonged. This was where they could come not only for comfort but for a dose of reality. The other parents understood their feelings and gently guided them over time toward a more realistic assessment of their child. The healing was demonstrated by Paul and Diane's eventual ability to laugh and make jokes.

Perhaps because Paul was beginning to feel better, he decided to come to me for private therapy to "conquer his demons of guilt." Paul frequently stated in the group that he felt haunted that God was punishing him, but he didn't know why. Therapy revealed some astonishing information for which neither Paul nor I was prepared.

Paul grew up the youngest of 10 children in a Catholic family. He was groomed to become the priest in his family, but as a young man in Jesuit school, he began to doubt his commitment to the life of a priest. He realized that what he really wanted was to be a husband and father. He received counseling from the head priest, who agreed that he should give up the idea and pursue the life he really desired.

This disappointed his family, but they soon understood and came around to giving him their blessings. Paul couldn't help feeling guilty about letting down his family, but eventually he discovered his talent for designing movie sets and set off to make a name for himself.

At the same time he met and married Diane, the love of his life. Life was proceeding well for him when she became pregnant. The pregnancy wasn't easy for Diane, and the delivery was even tougher. Everything went wrong, but their son Robert managed to pull through. Robert entered the hospital many times over the course of the next few years, each time fighting for his life. With each hospitalization, Paul's guilt increased.

In therapy, Paul and I revisited all the reasons why he felt God was punishing him. Although Paul adored his son and anguished over him, he nevertheless felt that he created an imperfect child because of something he'd done. When we examined the possibility that he might feel guilty about giving up the priesthood, he felt he'd worked through that with his family and with his mentor priest. No matter how hard we tried, we couldn't come up with any evidence leading to anything he had done to feel so guilty.

But one day after being in therapy for some time, he was talking about his childhood and where he'd lived. In describing his home and property on the bluffs overlooking the ocean in Northern California, he talked about a little friend with whom he played everyday. They loved to roll down a grassy hill toward the bluffs. Suddenly, as he was telling me about this pleasant experience, Paul's face registered shock and he became immediately pale. I thought he was ill.

After minutes passed, he began to sob. He suddenly remembered what had caused him such devastating guilt. When he finally could speak, he recalled a shocking story about the little girl who was his best friend. They were playing together one day when she rolled down the hill and kept going over the bluff where he could no longer see her. He was too afraid to look over the bluff, so he ran home. He never told anyone about this experience even when they asked him about her.

Only four years old, he felt too scared and guilty to say anything about what'd happened. Even though the girl's body was found at the bottom of the bluff, no one ever thought Paul had anything to do with the incident. He now realized he'd been carrying this burden with him for years, believing he was responsible for his childhood friend's death.

Decades later, after having his own child, Paul transferred this guilt to his son, thinking that God had punished him. It was about this time that Robert entered the hospital again, but this time he failed to survive. His funeral was so sad, but sweet and pure and attended by all of the parents in the group. Robert was finally out of pain and suffering.

Several months later, Paul and Diane had some fertility tests done because of previous difficult pregnancies and many miscarriages. They discovered that Robert's condition was due to genetic factors and that his parents were never fated to have a healthy child. A few years later, after recovering from their stressful period, Paul and Diane adopted a healthy little boy, and their life, at last, became more normalized, though, of course, they retained some battle scars. However, the guilt disappeared and now they're dealing with life's ups and downs just like everyone else.

## Chapter 10

# Lessons from a Lifetime of Service

"Only to the extent that we expose ourselves over
and over again to annihilation, can that
which is indestructible be found in us."

*—Pema Chodron*

*O*nce exposed to pain, most of us can find our strength over time, but we seldom realize this initially. In learning to accept what we cannot change—for instance, the child with the disability who can't be fixed—we ultimately must face ourselves. The healing comes from accepting this truth and the grief and misery that accompany it. Eventually, we accept the reality that we can't control everything that happens. And with that acceptance comes a discovery: Not only are we not destroyed, but, in fact, we're stronger.

No one passes through life without trauma or anguish. Turmoil is inescapable. And whether the crisis is loss of loved ones, ill health of family members, divorce or financial difficulties, the reactions are pretty similar: feelings of isolation, helplessness and depression. Yet we all have different styles of dealing with such trauma. Some take action to do something, anything, to keep feelings at bay. Others shut down, too petrified to move in any direction. Many come through their experiences wiser; others lose their way and become bitter.

In this chapter I'm going to, first, outline some General Observations I've noted while working with so many parents and children. Then I'll delve more deeply into Parents, Siblings, Extended Family, Placement, Parents' and Children's Rights, and Benchmarks on a Rocky Road Toward Balance, which describes the stages parents often go through. Finally, I end with my thoughts on The Biggest Asset, the single best attribute you can bring to your family and yourself.

The families with whom I've worked have taught me volumes about strength and endurance, about hope and dreams, about resiliency and never giving up. My hope is that by distilling some of the lessons I've learned, you, the reader, will be able to minimize—but, I'm sure, not eliminate—the grief. And, it's hoped, you'll find, sooner rather than later, the inner strength that will get you through any appalling experience.

# Six General Observations about Families

**1. Every family is unique.** How the parents respond to a child with a disability depends more on the parents' attitude about disability than on the actual severity of the disability. I've often heard spouses express opposite views of their child—that is, for instance, the father may accept the child as he or she is, a gift and a wonderful lesson for the whole family to embrace while the mother/wife expresses her sadness, worries about her child, and fears she isn't equal to the challenge. For her, this child isn't a gift but a burden, even though she loves her child. And in this case, the dad who's actively involved with his children considers the child first, and the disability second.

Both parents might agree to do what is necessary to help their child, but Mom is more tenacious in her search to uncover a cure (even if there isn't one) while Dad is more concerned with the child's comfort zone, place in life, and self-esteem than he is about finding a cure. So these parents operate from two different perspectives, one from acceptance and one from denial. The meaning of the child's disability is different for each, emanating from self-views. When crises occur, these parents often find themselves constantly at odds, debating what to do and how far to go to help their child's condition.

How, then, can these differences be reconciled? Time, patience, respect, and willingness are required for parents to listen to and take in each other's feelings. This occurs in families whose love and respect of each other supersedes all else. These parents seek a middle ground to help their child. They respect one another's approach as different—but not necessarily better or worse.

In situations where one spouse is uninvolved, it puts added pressure on the one already consumed with the caretaking and decision-making. The uninvolved parent is generally so unhappy about his/her child's disability that he/she escapes through work, drug of choice, or activities outside the home. If these differences become so intense as to create marital problems, then a family counselor is needed to help them try to work through their problems.

Unfortunately, these parents are often so consumed with anguish about their child, or guilty about their lack of involvement, that they're the last ones to call for help. Both claim they don't have enough time to see a counselor. By then, a pattern has developed: The less-involved parent leaves all decisions and most concerns up to the parent who is involved with the child, causing further resentment and isolation between the spouses.

Families need honesty, balance and objectivity—"HBO"— in their lives in order not to crumble under the weight of their problems. Having someone nearby to listen to them is a step toward healthy adjustment. Whether a friend, counselor, or another parent going through similar experiences, it's crucial to have someone be there (as I had in the early days) to provide reassurance and perhaps offer other perspectives.

At the very least, that reduces the sense of isolation. A mom in our group told me:

> Just once, I wish a friend would say to me, "I can't imagine how hard it is for you to have to deal with this on your own. It must be so tough to have to pretend with your friends that everything is fine and proceeding smoothly for your child, and putting on a happy face all the time." Friends are so happy when you can report progress your child is making, but they really don't want to face or hear the truth of what you're really experiencing. I can't blame them; that's just the way it is. Coming to the parent group gives me a chance to let my hair down and be honest with myself and others. It has been a tremendous help for my marriage.

As mentioned, the meaning that disability holds for parents is more crucial than the degree of the disability. If a child's disability is on the cusp so that the child appears more typical, that parent may worry more because the child tries so hard to fit in but is socially left out. Yet the parent of another, more severely involved child who's in a wheelchair might accept the reality of what he or she will be able to do in life. I've seen several young adults with severe disablities surprise everyone and go on to graduate from college, despite minimal expectations for them. Their parents clearly saw their ability above and beyond their disabilities.

When parents have a place to come together to talk, their problems seem less challenging. I've not done a study on parent groups, but my 30 years of working with parents and their children leads me to believe that those who participate in support groups make quicker and better adjustments and accept their reality simply because they feel supported and less alone.

**2. The best thing frightened parents can do is face their feelings and admit their frustrations.** It takes time for them to learn to accept their feelings as natural, neither wrong nor right. Parents get into trouble when their expectations of themselves are too high. They can't possibly be as perfect as they expect to be.

Real control comes when they're able to honestly accept their fallibilities, feel their raw emotions, and deal with them. Parents need to let go of an all-or-nothing way of thinking that sets them up for failure. "Should" statements lead to guilt when parents feel compelled to do things because they should, not because they want to.

Paying attention only to the negative and not to the positive keeps you from seeing the positive attributes in yourself, your family and your child with the disability. A sure sign of this is ever-constant, consuming anger toward others or toward the injustices of the system serving their children. Nothing is ever that bad!

Such overreactions are exhausting and prevent parents from looking at the reality of their circumstances and from helping their children. They become so swept up by hopelessness and rage that there's little left over for the child.

**3. Disability affects not only the parent and child but the whole family**. Families working together experience a real opportunity. Siblings, for instance, can learn deep compassion and caring if parents consider the sibling's emotional needs as important as the needs of their child with a disability. This requires a balance in taking an active role between the sibling's activities and the activities of the special-needs child. The sibling must feel safe in expressing his/her feelings and having his/her needs met.

In most healthy families, children learn to take turns, and that's true, too, for the family with the child with a disability. Families can learn to carry out these goals through problem-solving and communication training from therapists who're experienced in helping families adjust to their situation.

**4. A child's emotional health depends on the emotional health of the family**. If the family is to survive and function optimally, parents must give as much time, attention, and affection to themselves, their spouses, and their other children as they do to their child with a disability.

**5. Parents don't have to be geniuses or have all the answers**. But they do need to expend effort, trust their own judgment, think creatively and set realistic goals for their family, including taking care of themselves. If they learn to follow these suggestions, they will gain insight, self assurance, and the ability to turn potential tragedy into strength and meaning.

**6. Parents must learn that new dreams can be created.** A balance in your family's life is crucial and attainable. Most important, realize there's a person of worth living within the soul of your child with a disability. Open your heart to that soul. Try to not allow his/her disability loom larger than your child.

Immigrants bring to the American melting pot their own ideas and attitudes. I've worked with parents who come from countries around the world and who have brought with them different feelings about their children with disabilities. It's been a learning experience for me to listen to their ideas and to help them problem-solve in their families. They love their children, as most parents do, but sometimes their families of origin turn their backs on the child with a disability and his/her parent because their culture tells them the child has cast shame on their family.

It's most difficult at first for these parents not to take on those familial attitudes. But after working with them for a while, I see them begin to feel less shunned and more equipped to handle the experience without allowing their relatives' attitudes to affect their parenting.

## *Parents*

Of all the challenges life presents us, nothing is more important than our role as a parent, yet it's the very task for which we're least prepared. Research has shown that the earliest years in a child's life are when future life patterns are being developed most rapidly. During these critical years, parents are the major influence in their child's life. As the children are rapidly developing and gaining awareness of themselves in their world, so too, should their parents be learning. When parents learn how children develop, they have more confidence in their own abilities to cope with problems that might arise during the formative years. When parents discover that their child is ill or has a serious disability, their fear causes a feeling of groundlessness. This can result in parents busying themselves and making themselves frantic, instead of patiently waiting for more information as to how to proceed.

Parents of children with special needs/disabilities are usually no more ready or special than other parents to meet challenges that face them once the disability is discovered. Society often demands they become superhuman to cope suddenly with new and confusing feelings regarding their child and their new role as parents.

When I was young and caring for Dana, I had no clue about child development. Like most young parents then, I was dependent on the pediatrician for all information. I was afraid to make a move without first consulting him. I didn't trust my own judgment, yet there were huge gaps in my learning and in his providing sufficient information. With the onslaught of managed health care, doctors have even less time for their patients. Because of this, more parents have educated themselves about their child's disability and are now generally more knowledgeable and less afraid to step up to assume their rights.

## Regular people

One of the things that Dana taught me and that my years as a therapist confirmed, is that parents of a child with disabilities are regular people, who can, and who usually do, manage their challenges. And once they get through the initial tough times, they manage with grace. That isn't to say it's ever easy, even when parents are experiencing a period of relative calmness. It's a tough job to raise a child with disabilities. But it's do-able for most, but not all.

When others say you, the parent, are "a miracle worker," and that they could never accomplish what you have done, most are secretly grateful they don't have to experience what you've gone through.

When I first became a therapist working with families, I believed my work was to help them avoid the pitfalls that we as parents stumbled into. I also felt that I needed to rescue others from feeling the emotional pain they were experiencing, the same pain that my husband and I felt about our child. I soon realized that one cannot avoid feeling pain, nor was it my right to rescue them from their right to feel whatever they were feeling. I also realized that not everyone necessarily felt the same way. No one had the right to tell them how to be.

They had to follow their own paths. Instead, the best I could do was to extend a hand to those traveling the same or similar paths and listen to their stories. My job was to meet them, and respect where they were, by supporting them as they moved from darkness to light. I saw my job as helping them better understand themselves and the process they were going through to get to growth and healing. This helped them understand that they weren't crazy or wrong for feeling and thinking the way they did.

# Fears of suicide

When a few parents managed to confess to me their fears of suicide, I held no judgment of them and took their fears very seriously. I knew they saw suicide as a way to end their terrible pain. In time, they began to relax, and the talk of death subsided as they gained a greater knowledge of what they were going through. I knew their death wishes had to be frightening and real to them. All I could do was reassure them, and let them know that I was close by. Reality-testing was critical for parents experiencing these frightening fantasies, and I saw in them usually not a serious mental illness but an inordinate amount of fear, pain, and negative self-judgment.

They were scared to death that they couldn't take good enough care of their child with the disability and do everything else as well. We worked hard together to help them gain confidence in their parenting and decision-making skills. So many parents felt paralyzed by irrational fears. But I would ask them: "What's the worst thing that could happen if your fears materialized?" That would force them to state their worst fantasies out loud. Once those were uttered for both of us to hear, they were surprised that their fears became less frightening. From this experience, they came to realize that they had allowed the disability to loom larger than the child, which overwhelmed them. Their spirits would lift if I could help them learn to figuratively step out of their circumstances even for a moment, to regroup and gain some distance from their reactions. Once they tackled that objective of replacing their frightening feelings with reality, they could move literally to a new place of relief and acceptance, allowing them to carry on with their lives in general.

# Building confidence

Parents of children with disabilities have little time for pleasure. Too often, they're so overwhelmed, they have difficulty making decisions. Yet, they must learn to trust themselves enough to go slowly and gain confidence in their own resources and skills. Taking time to make decisions builds confidence. This confidence allows them to take better control of a situation rather than to allow themselves to be overwhelmed by the situation.

I've always tried to encourage individuality and confidence in parents by helping them focus on the unique gifts of their child. When we communicate to our children in our daily interactions, we're also communicating our attitudes about them. They, in turn, develop attitudes about themselves and the world. One of my objectives was to help parents gain insight into their children by seeing their abilities and behaviors as they really are, not how they think they are, or how they want them to be.

Some parents initially see their child with a disability as being extremely limited, without any real potential. But after parents become educated in basic child development, they can better understand their child by learning how children develop in stages. This understanding allows the parents to help their child reach the next stage, albeit at the child's pace. Although there's no real timetable, children with disabilities (unless the disability is so debilitating, like Dana's) will reach certain milestones of development with therapeutic intervention. Without this intervention, their chances are more limited, but not impossible.

## High and low expectations

Many parents have told me that they have trouble being objective and find it difficult to set limits for their children. Some, myself included, tended to give in to their child because our expectations were less than they should have been. Yet there's nothing more obnoxious than an overindulged child, especially one with a disability. He or she has never had any kind of expectations set for them, so how do they learn to live in the world?

Remember Helen Keller as a wild child who had no restrictions placed on her until her beloved Annie saved her? Generally speaking, overindulged children have overwhelmed parents. These parents feel guilty about their own feelings and pressure from well meaning family members, who have low expectations for their child, thus creating helpless or acting out children. Fear of reprisal and criticism compels the parent to answer every beck and call, robbing their child of any opportunity to grow and develop independence and self worth.

At the root of this problem is the fine line between acceptance and denial. Parents often err by feeling so sorry for their child that they overprotect him or her, or aspire far beyond the child's abilities.

For example, when a child's walking is physically regressing, that's understandably tough on the parents. Some have so much difficulty accepting the regression that they push their child even harder to walk. Scared to death that the child will live his or her entire life in a wheelchair, the parents may keep pushing the child beyond his/her capabilities.

When the parent learns that their child will never walk; it's a devastating blow. As long as they could keep their child walking, the parents could see their child living independently and having a bright future, but once the wheelchair becomes the only means of transportation, the dreams and expectations feel blown away, like the loss they felt when first discovering their child had a disability. Though their plans for their child had been derailed, they still can't lose the ability to dream and hope. Once they have to wrestle with the reality of their child's real disabilities, they have to find ways other than walking to ensure that their child can have an independent and happy future, just like Caroline in our first family story.

On the other hand, some parents have unrealistically low expectations. Afraid and at a loss as to what to do, they fail to give the child proper direction. They give up on their child, right from the beginning, without trying anything, regardless of the degree of disability. Sometimes, their cultural attitudes affect their reactions to having a child with a disability, especially when disability has been shunned. Their reality is skewed because they are weighed down by never-ending shame, guilt, depression and anger, and can't really see the child within. This kind of situation is tough on family relationships and often causes bitter arguments between husband and wife with the potential breakdown of the family unit.

In my program, for some children, the degree of disability made a difference in their ability to learn, and we helped those parents find more effective ways to take the helm. Whenever necessary, we'd make home visits to see how the child acted, either by crying or being more willful in his/her home rather than at the program. When this kind of behavior would present itself in our classroom, we could intervene by modeling behavior for the parent, thereby teaching Mom or Dad new ways to reach their child.

For those children who made excruciatingly slow progress, the parents felt frustrated after spending incredible time and effort working with their children. The return rate of success was insignificant compared to the huge investment parents made in their children's development. Nevertheless, the parents continued on, even though they at times they felt disappointed or sorry for their kids and for themselves. But when the success was measurable, parents celebrated and then worked even harder to extend the progress. There were some parents who believed their child was incapable of doing anything. So they coddled their children and expected nothing in return. These children, who could have at least developed to their potential, never had a chance. Fortunately, this wasn't true in the majority of families that I saw.

Disability affects family life in many ways, some of which are destructive. There was often a heavy toll on the siblings in the family, due to the parents' over-consuming attention being paid to the child with the disability. The mothers who spent all their time trying to meet the entire family's needs usually did so at their own expense. They never stopped to take care of themselves. Consequently, having little time to rest and heal, how could mothers feel calm and assured that they would make clear decisions? The fathers who could not spend time due to other demands, often felt left out and abandoned by their wives. Little opportunity remained for spouses to spend quality time with each other. Some parents held secret feelings of blame toward each other for having a child with a disability. .

Out of shame, embarrassment, an inability to trust or an unwillingness to share their experiences, some parents of children with disabilities still have difficulty finding someone to talk to or making their physicians aware of their predicament.

## Siblings

I could've written an entire book on siblings of children with disabilities, but many wonderful books have already been written on the subject. So, instead, I've chosen to shed some light on typically occurring patterns affecting siblings' reactions to disability, both generally and specifically.

When a child with a disability is born, every family member's life is permanently altered. The adjustment period in a family's acceptance is different for each family; it can be a slow, difficult process, or a relatively brief one that's more easily accepted.

Societal demands and pressures become more complicated for the family with a child with a disability. Naturally, the siblings are affected by everything going on in their home. A sibling who's experiencing a major transition in his or her life will have compounded worries when a brother or sister with the disability is hospitalized, or critically ill. He or she might also be experiencing a time of crisis, or experiencing jubilation over a special occasion, such as a graduation, and the parents might not be able to share the experience because of the attention they're focusing on the other child with the disability.

In these instances, there doesn't seem to be enough time for everyone to have their needs met; most often, the siblings are the ones left behind. Understandably, this can make them resent their parents and then feel guilty about that resentment. If the parents aren't sensitive to their children's individual needs, the sibling is primed for acting out.

# John's situation

As it happened, John, one of the fathers in my parent group, told us he was a neglected sibling, although he didn't have a sibling with a disability, as we define it. His older brother, Skip, was sickly from an early age. As the younger, healthier brother, John was expected to be the good child, stay out of trouble and carry out various duties in the household because his mother was too caught up with her older son's asthmatic condition. His father worked all the time, and when he came home, many arguments ensued between the parents, often ending with his dad retiring early, shutting the door behind him.

The message John got loud and clear was to stay away and keep out of trouble. Though Skip's asthma curiously disappeared, Skip later developed a severe drug addiction. Then John's parents felt guilty and gave Skip money whenever he asked, which was frequent. At no time did John remember his parents doing anything special for him, especially not taking a particular interest in his activities. All they did was give him money to entertain himself. He felt as if he was being paid off to stay away and not bother them.

In fact, their literal comment to him was, "You're normal; you don't need us like your brother needs us. He's sick." No matter what John did, or how much he accomplished, he felt that his parents continuously shut the door in his face. They felt relieved they didn't have to worry about him. Well into their 40s, the brothers continued to receive different treatment from their parents. John determinedly went on to become a self-supporting, successful pharmacist, while Skip was still being bailed out of jail and treated as if he were still the ill and helpless child by his parents.

John came to see me for therapy when his first-born son was discovered to have a major developmental disability. His reactions to his son brought up old feelings and memories of his earlier experiences, but this time his child was the one affected. John was also bothered about his parents' lack of attention to his son. He could've continued to anguish over their disinterest, but realized in therapy they weren't capable of giving him what he wanted. He knew that just because he had a child with a disability, they wouldn't suddenly change into the loving and attentive parents and grandparents that he craved.

He decided to give up longing for their attention. He went through a period of grieving, and the adjustment was difficult, but he was able to have a different relationship with his parents. He no longer focused on the love he never received. Instead, he focused on his own family as he and his wife courageously moved on to have three more healthy children.

He made sure that his younger children would not undergo the painful rejection he'd felt. His struggle was valiant, taking extra pains to give at least equal attention to his other children, however difficult. John managed to stay conscious of his children's welfare because he knew what it was like to be a sibling neglected by his parents.

# Challenges

The family with the child with a disability is vulnerable to outside as well as internal pressures that can leave them feeling isolated, fearful, and lonely. They're challenged by experiences that both stress and strengthen them. Many learn from these experiences that they're survivors and can turn a potentially damaging experience into a rewarding one.

How parents interpret and accept their child's disability has a direct effect on their typically developing children as well. Parents who maintain ongoing, honest, and open communication with their children help reduce any disturbing feelings their typical children might experience. Children often fear they might become disabled themselves, or that their future children might have disabilities. The typically developing child might try to always be the good child, thinking he or she doesn't have the right to feel angry over a lack of attention.

If parents don't have the time or the capacity to listen to or attend to their other children's' needs, the sibling's resentful feelings will grow into a deeper sense of rage. In that kind of situation, it takes professional input to help parents learn how to better deal with their children.

When parents treat all of their children fairly, siblings more readily accept their family's circumstances. The siblings are more apt to experience real joy over their disabled brother's or sister's accomplishments and be more willing to help them. It's usually these children who grow into adults who've accepted their brother's or sister's disability as a natural part of life and who show compassion and feelings of warmth and respect for others.

I've also seen some families in which a sibling is the model child saddled with unrealistic expectations. This may be unconsciously encouraged by a parent who needs the sibling to compensate for the child with the disability. It's particularly disturbing to witness a child cater to his or her sister with a disability over and above his or her own needs, or to agonize over accomplishing perfect grades to please the parents.

The drive to succeed and to be "good" can propel a child into later problems if the parent pays attention only to the child's accomplishments. I've seen this occur in professional families, especially in the medical community, when highly educated parents feel very disappointed and bewildered by their disabled child's limitations. Some professionals feel personally wounded and disappointed at having a child with developmental disabilities. I've also seen this in families from different cultures in which people with disabilities are not generally accepted.

Parents sometimes load expectations on the typical child who can make the parents feel better about themselves. Parents who feel as if their child with a disability is a negative reflection of them may count on the "good child" to perform, thus relieving their shame and embarrassment. This child becomes the caretaker for the parents, always dedicated to making them feel good about their parenting.

This was true in our family, even though Dana was living elsewhere. Our son Scott, when very young, was expected to achieve goals we unconsciously set for him to make up for Dana, even though Dana was not living at home. How sad that then we had no clue. Scott's drive to be the best in everything he did became obvious to us when it was already too late for us to do anything about it. The best we could do was to talk about it with him after he was grown. Sibling reaction has everything to do with the parental adjustment and acceptance of the child with the disability. Everyone—whether a highly functioning parent, or not—has difficulty adjusting to parenting a child with a disability. It takes patience, strength, and fortitude, and time to find resources and support to help these parents feel they're on the right path.

It's understandable that siblings would feel threatened and insecure at the beginning of their parents' journey to accept their disabled child. Naturally, a good marriage with positive communication and close family relationships helps foster interaction and diminishes the stresses of having a sister or brother with a disability.     Positive attitudes of both parents strongly influence all the children in the family. But for those who are less lucky in their relationships, it's imperative for these families to seek support and direction from a counselor experienced in the field of family and disability counseling.

## The sibling group experience

The siblings' responses to their brother or sister with disabilities depend also on the age, gender and birth order of the sibling. For example, the older sister tends to be a caretaker while the closer in age but younger sib often takes on the role of an older sibling. Whatever the role, whatever the family dynamics, many groups and workshops exist to help siblings understand and better adjust to their situations. These can help create a social network for the sibs, assist them in feeling supported and heard.

United Cerebral Palsy, Down Syndrome Parents, and the Autistic Society are among the organizations with ongoing sibling groups. Other support information can be found online under the heading of "Siblings of Children with Disabilities" or in various university libraries and local disability organizations.

The sib groups generally are not psychotherapy, but rather, therapeutic places for brothers and sisters to come together and share experiences. Often they're conducted in a play environment. Through symbolic play, conversation and fun, the sibs begin to learn that their brother or sister with the disability is a person first and should be treated accordingly. They also learn that whatever negative feelings they might have are more common than what they expect. This instills in the siblings, and in their parents as well, more realistic attitudes and greater understanding.

The group experience provides an opportunity to teach siblings to be more accepting of themselves and, ultimately, of their situation. It also helps them realize they're not alone. The sharing of problems and information helps siblings recognize their unique talents and abilities as participating members of their families. This is a great opportunity for all kids, and the younger they are, the better chance for them to adjust. In these cases, the sib groups are a godsend. At the very least, if a group or therapist is not available, having someone, anyone, who is respected by the child, a good family friend, or a teacher should be available for the sib to share personal feelings. This is critical because most children don't have the willingness, the ability, or the opportunity to do much soul-searching without the sharing experience.

# The Extended Family

It's a lucky child, especially a child with disabilities, who's surrounded by loving family members. That child is celebrated by her family with love and respect and is valued for who she is, not for what she should've been. The family forms a strong supportive system around her.

Grandparents, aunts, and uncles can either be wonderful additions to the family member with disabilities, or they can be pretty miserable. Reactions range anywhere from self-sacrificing to generally disinterested. Whatever those reactions, they all have a critical impact on the family with children with disabilities. And I've seen them all.

Interestingly, people often assume roles in a family and play out their roles long after they've moved out of the family home. Those roles—such as dominance, submission, avoidance and caretakers— can carry on into their new families, unless the person has learned through therapy or experience that this role is inappropriate and unnecessary.

Parents of children with disabilities feel their relatives' responses keenly and react accordingly. When extended family members demonstrate caring and concern by respecting the parents' decisions and offering support, everyone is happy. But when relatives criticize how the parents handle their situation, or when they make critical comments about the child, bad feelings result and an already stressful situation worsens. Because the relatives aren't there 24/7, they aren't qualified to know what goes on behind closed doors.

If parents are filled with self-doubt and worry, they might buy into the general criticisms expressed by their families, causing them even more stress. The situation can be further aggravated when grandparents, aunts or uncles spoil or infantilize the child (against the parents' wishes) when the parents are trying so hard to set boundaries for their child. It becomes difficult to stand up to a grandparent who has been an authority figure for so many years, regardless how wrong he or she might be.

The parents of a child with a disability, just like all parents, have many things on their plate to worry about. The last thing they should have to fear is criticism from the extended family members. Parents sometimes give away their power as if they're still the young children in the family. But healthy parents know they're in charge and are objective enough to take what is good from their extended family members and when to discard the critical.

## More about Placement

The time may come, as it did for me, when parents must place their child in a residential setting because the child can no longer live at home. This is a tough decision, for sure, but one which parents can reach realistically. The previous discussion in Chapter 8 about placement didn't mention that parents can choose the kind of home, location, levels, and types of disabilities of the children living there and select the caretakers for their older children. Despite the feelings of loss that may come up for parent and child during this time, the anxiety is greatly lessened if the placement is felt to be the next appropriate step for everybody concerned.

Yet so many parents are overprotective and fear taking this step that the child ends up at home well into adulthood, even though the parent can no longer provide the same kinds of stimulation and activities that the child would get in a group home. Of course, if the situation isn't an improvement, if the child cannot adjust, he or she can always return to the family home. Or the parents might seek another, more suitable place for him or her to live.

Among the problems that create difficulties for parents caring for their child in the family home are the severity of the child's disability, non-supportive hostile professionals, inadequate resources in their community, lack of appropriate social stimulation, and demands of the parents' workplace. These can have a direct effect on the quality of life for the family. Parents may feel devalued by a non-accepting community, which can result in the parent feeling stigmatized and unwittingly rejecting their own child with the disability.

## Parents' and Children's Rights

I see today's parents becoming more active and secure in seeking services for their child's needs because they realize their rights. More recognize that if there's to be a change, it's up to them. As a result, they're creating changes in the system, albeit slowly. Although far from perfect, this collective parental voice is making a difference for many.

These challenges to the agencies has had a positive impact because more parents are refusing to just go away when services are not rendered. In times past, parents wouldn't think of standing up to professionals to assert their rights. Instead, they would leave feeling defeated and lost.

In certain instances, the courts have supported the parental requests through fair hearings. With the passage of the American Disabilities Act (ADA) in 1990, the rights of citizens with disabilities were supposed to have been secured, but a lag developed because of a lack of funds and the inability of the government to enforce the ADA, which has resulted in parents seeking private lawsuits to obtain their rights.

As parental activism increases and succeeds in securing rights for their children, it has begun to permeate throughout society, including the indigent and other underserved populations. Even though the problems of poverty continue, lower-socioeconomic parents are becoming more aware and actively pursuing what's needed for their child. Now that inclusion is at the forefront, parents of children with and without disabilities want their children to participate together, regardless of social status.

## Having the right team

In the past, when parents cried or broke down in the physician's office, it was unusual for a doctor to do anything more than to offer a few words of solace. Mostly, the physician would rush off to the next patient.  Even   though   doctors truly believe they're dedicated experts in caring for children with disabilities, many still haven't been trained sufficiently to understand parents' feelings or reactions.

Many parents, though, are getting smarter, insisting that their doctors listen to them. But not all doctors are capable of hearing.

After all, psychology isn't given a major role in medical school. Further, I think many doctors believed they had to separate themselves from their emotions in order to carry on. It isn't as if they didn't care. They just could not allow themselves to become too close or vulnerable to parents or to the situation. I'm sure they thought that if they did, how could they do their job?

In reality, doctors don't need to have all the answers. But they do need to show they care. By taking time and asking, "Do you have any questions?" or "How can I help you?" or by saying "Tell me more about how you feel," doctors can do much to bridge the gap between them and the parents of children with disabilities. Learning to listen is as important as supplying answers.

Parents have gotten stronger, taking on the role of teaching physicians that their child is part of the whole picture, that the family's feelings and concerns are critical to the child's welfare. Increasingly, parents are now seen by professionals as being experts because of the knowledge they have about their children. After years of resistance, the medical community today has generally come around to recognize the parent as part of the team rather than apart from the team, which ultimately aids the doctor in helping the child. Now in the era of managed health care, doctors are even more limited in their service, which puts the burden more squarely on the parents' shoulders.

Unfortunately, some parents who may have limited language skills or are unsophisticated feel intimidated and think they lack the right to question or criticize the "expert." These parents need to have someone, perhaps an advocate, to help them comprehend and better deal with their situation.

Some parents, depending on their culture in which they were raised, feel shame about having a child with a disability. They feel that their child negatively reflects on them as parents and that it's their fault that their child has a disability. Again, an advocate can help dispel this myth. Once parents come to realize the situation isn't their fault, they're more able to accept their new reality and seek the best treatment possible. When doctors include parents on their team, the opportunities for improvement only grow. I wish that I had felt more proficient about myself in those early days.

## Benchmarks on a Rocky Road toward Balance

It's been said that the process of adjustment that parents of children with disabilities go through can be likened to the stages of death and dying famously described by Dr. Elisabeth Kubler-Ross. Except, of course, in this case, not real death but rather the death of the parents' dream is the issue. When their child isn't what they had planned for, it's a terrible blow. When that happens, they experience: Denial, Anger, Bargaining, Excessive Worry (my addition), Depression and, finally, Acceptance.

These stages might better be described as "states of emotion" because they're really not a progression and may be revisited from time to time in any order. Parents move in differing ways through these states, which aren't as smooth and orderly as they sound. Rather, they might be messy and fraught with anxiety over a long period. But, generally, the process leads parents to a place where they have an increased ability to care for their children and make better, more realistic decisions for their child as well as to create new dreams.

Over the many years I've worked with families, I've noticed some of the natural reactions parents have as they raise their children with disabilities. Even though the parent feels as if he/she is the only one in the world who has these feelings, most parents experience them. And, I believe, these feelings can be viewed as a rocky road toward health, a journey toward realizing they will be, in fact, survivors.

## Shock— "This can't be happening to us!"

This moment occurs when one first learns about the child's diagnosis. Inevitably, the question comes up, "How can this be true?" A sense of paralysis sets in, and what seems like a total lack of control leaves the parent asking, "Why me? Is my life ruined? How will I be able to manage?"

These thoughts can create a chain reaction of dark feelings as the truth sets in that the child's disability could forever upset the entire family. Many parents have likened their feelings to drowning or being swept away by life-threatening feelings of remorse and fear. Unlike measles or mumps, disability isn't likely to disappear, but it's important to recognize there's no-one-size-fits-all response to disability. Parents' reactions vary widely.

Parents of mildly affected children may suffer as much as parents of children with severe disabilities. This has to do with parental feelings and attitudes, and, again, the meaning that disability has for the parents. Some cannot accept anything less than perfection in their child. Shock about this imperfect child may range from super- aggressive, angry responses to complete immobility or rejection of all outside help.

It's best not to fight these feelings. As with a shock to the body, it won't pass if one overreacts by trying to keep moving. The longer you fight, the longer it takes to heal. This period often involves obsessing about the child's future, imagining (without any evidence) the very worst. Most often the very worst fantasies never develop. But, during this frantic time, many fight their sense of helplessness by overreacting and running to doctors or doing anything they can to ward off the helplessness.

These parents are hell-bent to find a cure and become panicked if any path is left unexplored. I've helped parents recognize that none of the panic or bouts of sorrow are as terrible as the first moments of discovery. Parents can take heart that in surviving this period, they'll survive again and again, realizing that each round will be easier for them and their family to endure.

## Guilt - "What did I do wrong?"

It's a rare parent who doesn't shoulder the blame at some time for having a child with a disability. Guilt is one of the toughest obstacles to overcome. It's also a waste of valuable time.

Parents can convince themselves they're at fault for creating the disability. They can reach into the past and find something they did when they were younger that might've caused this. Or they can reach deep into their subconscious and become guilty over having "bad" thoughts about something or someone.

225

None of this makes sense to anyone but to the one who feels the guilt. It serves the purpose of offering a rationalization for something that occurs randomly. The idea seems to be: Any explanation is better than none because it's very tough to accept randomness. What's bad about this guilt is it can lead to self-harming actions or cause the person to shut down entirely, incapacitated by overwhelming self-hate.

I've seen guilt overwhelm parents. They put insurmountable pressure on themselves to constantly pursue the right answer to fix their child, and if it doesn't come, the parents are depressed and feel like failures. These parents always find questions to pursue and always find some kind of answer, though not necessarily the right answer. But they won't rest until everything on earth has been explored and explained fully. What are the chances of that ever happening?

One can ultimately ease symptoms of guilt by recognizing it and forgiving oneself. It's crucial to self-forgive in order to move on. This can be done with the help of religious or psychological counseling. If parents allow themselves this gift, Dad and Mom will learn they're worthwhile and will learn to take better care of themselves and their other children as well. They'll learn that all family members deserve equal time, and they'll take small steps to ensure that everyone can cherish small daily joys, like taking a bath, reading, spending time alone to regroup, and enjoying positive time together. In this way, the family members feel better about themselves and are more apt to take turns helping out, which results in real teamwork.

If families aren't attentive to each other, one member—typically the mother—feels obligated to do everything, resenting the rest of the family for not assisting. In these cases, embitterment overwhelms family members and results in strong resistance and defiant behaviors, making quality of life almost impossible for them. These families can end up going in different directions, feeling isolated rather than becoming stronger and more bonded to each other.

## Denial -"Everything is fine."

At the beginning, a certain amount of denial is "normal" and almost necessary for recovery. It provides time to gather strength because parents aren't ready to handle their feelings regarding the truth. Denial is often tied to guilt because it denies angry feelings or blame that might be felt toward the child or spouse. Denial protects against falling apart when one first discovers the reality of the disability. Initially, it allows for hope. But if denial goes on for too long, it takes a terrible toll on the whole family.

The longer the parent keeps reality at bay, the more difficult the adjustment is for the child and the parent. I've known some parents who've lived in denial for many years, still hoping for a miracle that will make their child "normal." I know I did that early in Dana's life. In such cases, divorce rates are extremely high, with the one parent who's in denial living a painful and lonely existence. These parents forsake everything and everyone else in their lives, waiting for the magic to happen.

I knew a mother of a boy with severe disabilities who couldn't feed himself, partly because the mother treated him like an infant and fed him instead of teaching him to feed himself. She did everything for him and stopped taking him to therapy and classes because "they weren't helping him. I can help him more." I was very concerned about her situation because she infantilized her son and ignored the needs of her other child and her husband.

Her behavior suggested she was in serious need of psychotherapy, which I suggested but which she refused. When she spoke of her disabled son, she always spoke of him as her baby and in terms of when he would become "normal," which never happened. Clearly a very angry woman, she denied her feelings by babying her son and ultimately ended up living only with him, without the support of her husband and the other child because she closed them out.

Fifteen years passed (I'd lost touch with her) when she called me, crying hysterically. At first, I didn't remember her until she started to tell me about her son. She'd had just tried to feed her son, who was now 21, but he wouldn't accept any food. Instead, he spit the food out at her; she lost control and hit him across the face. After I got her to calm down, she told me. "Everything was the same, nothing had changed," except that now he was an adult exhibiting anger and frustration at her by rebelling in his very limited ways.

Her voice was strangely calm and quiet as she said to me, "I don't understand why he treated me so cruelly when all I have done is live for him. I have no one else in the world but him, and now he is turning away from me just like my husband did. Something inside me exploded when he spit at me, and I slapped him across his face for the very first time. I'll never do it again." Until he spit out the food at her, she still believed there was hope for his improvement and that she was the only one who could make it happen.

Her son, although very disabled, understood on some level that he was being prohibited by his mother to grow and develop to the best of his ability. The only way he could rebel was to spit food at her and, even then, her denial reigned. It wasn't long before he was moved from her home into a group home for young adults, both for his sake and because she could no longer emotionally or physically handle him. She finally had to give in, because he became too physically heavy for her to move him. This made her feel like a complete failure. This poor woman couldn't see beyond herself to effectively help him. The years of symbiotic attachment between them prevented them both from ever having a chance to live a quality life.

Whatever her real instincts, they were overshadowed by guilt and denial. If she'd been able to really see the situation without all of the negative self-judgment, everyone might have been saved from the terrible ordeal. (I tried to contact her recently, but she'd moved out of state.) Her mental illness prevented her from helping him develop. Such pathological denial can drive a parent to overcompensate for the child, insisting there is a "cure" around the corner.

Trying to fix the child at the expense of other family members disables the entire family. When parents are hell-bent to find a cure for their child at all costs, it generally results in financial ruin, a rise in divorce, alcoholism, and sometimes suicide when the cure doesn't appear. In the rush for a panacea, a parent in denial may sweep aside the siblings as well as the partner. Siblings act out either by being the perfect child, ignoring their own needs, or by doing emotional or physically injurious things to themselves or to others. Denial prevents us from facing our real feelings and dealing with them before we have become damaged in the process. It requires the letting go of all the fantasies and facing the real truth. Only then can the parents move beyond denial into the very healing phase: grieving.

## Grieving -"Loss of the ideal dream."

When the denial phase ends within a reasonable period of time, it allows the parent to grieve, which feels often frightening to parents. This is the time of recognition. This is when their dreams of an ideal child disappear, creating within them a deep sadness—sadness so dark, they feel all's lost. What parents don't realize is this mourning contains the seed of a breakthrough. All of the rage, guilt and denial have been swept away by the harsh and plain truth.

Although parents may feel stuck during this period because they're overwhelmed by sadness, they give up the frenzied search and ultimately gain the power to make correct decisions for their child. Their real child is there for them to see. At this point, they can now deal with the reality of their situation. It's the fortunate parent (although he or she may not feel fortunate) who's able to get to this point of realistic expectations.

For other parents who're so afraid of giving up their imagined power, guilt and denial nag at them as they continue to seek bigger and better solutions for their child. Their journey to this dark place is only temporary. I've supported many parents during this very low, mournful period of adjustment. The task is to help them understand it's not abnormal to feel depressed when their child attends birthday parties or goes to public places where other children are playing. This can be a harsh reminder that their child is delayed developmentally, and parents can't help comparing their child with the others who aren't disabled. It certainly doesn't help when others make remarks or stare at their children.

I knew a mom who would go up to the person who was staring at her child and tell the person, in a very nice way, all about her child, This seemed to alleviate her depression and isolation. By taking charge of the situation, she knew she changed another's perceptions, which gave her a feeling of strength and control.

Depression and sadness are tough and require support from professionals or other parents who have gone through this difficult, important time. This crucial support helps the parent move toward the reality phase, in which they can begin to see the child for his or her unique gifts, letting go of the pursuit of false realities.

## Reality – "Seeing the child for her unique gifts."

When disability no longer looms larger than the whole child, the family is free to experience the child more realistically. This is when each family member feels noticed and appreciated for who they are. If the child strives to succeed in walking or talking or even smiling at his/her parent, albeit late, the situation feels less bleak and hopeless. Parents experience the progress as triumphs. They celebrate every milestone, large or small.

Family members begin to see the child's idiosyncrasies as lovable; they appreciate their child's smile and wonderful innocence. Slowly, perhaps for the first time, healing has begun, and the child is finally enjoyed for who he or she is. In a giant step forward, Mom and Dad begin focusing less on "What did we do to deserve this?" and more on "How can we make the best of this situation?"

Life—good and bad—keeps happening to parents with children with and without disabilities. We realize, as parents, we can't control everything, no matter how hard we try. But we can control how we view our circumstances by dealing with what is. Once parents learn this, they're on the way toward being rehabilitated rather than debilitated. As the dark clouds lift, parents will find themselves doing more "normal" activities and noticing small joys like laughter and hugs. Everything in life becomes more appreciated.

Their child hasn't changed all that much but now fits into the family as a bona fide family member with all his/her individual quirks. Life has gotten lighter as the household is filled with more cheer. Parents and siblings alike recognize that they matter, too.

## Resiliency – "Bouncing back, giving back."

This is the stage when parents feel more active and ready to participate in their world, whether that's the world of disability or other activities. This is the time of strength and flexibility, when they no longer feel overshadowed by alienation and isolation. Parents have given up the notion that they've done something wrong, that they're being punished for evil thoughts or bad deeds. Very often, parents become advocates for their children and help other parents adjust to their new and similar situations. One of the most notable traits they exhibit is a sense of humor, as they finally stop trying to make sense out of a senseless situation.

## The Biggest Asset

When it's all said and done, your outlook is the most important asset in dealing with your child with disabilities. More than money and time spent, more than sheer will, more even than fervent hopes and prayers, attitude is what determines a family's success. Believe it or not, I've seen parents of children with severe disabilities handle their situation more effectively than parents of a child with a much lesser disability. What's more, I've seen parents with fewer financial resources function far better than rich ones.

Why is that? I think it's largely because these less financially secure parents, or parents of children with more severe disabilities, felt less internally impoverished than their counterparts who had more money and/or less of a disability to wrestle with.

As far as I can tell, these better attitudes seemed to emanate from their general outlook on life. Their inherent sense of self seemed to direct these parents in a realistic way toward realistic goals. Objectivity and balance served them well.

*Objectivity.* Objectivity promotes well-being because parents have a healthy distance between themselves and their children. When parents can't stop feeling so strongly identified with their child's disability, they experience the disability as if it's happened to them.

One wise parent said to me about his child, "No one is to blame. One has to accept that life's roads are filled with potholes. We didn't miss this one, but we will miss others. We accept that we must go on, because we have our whole family to think of."

*Balance*. They do everything they can for their child with the disability but not at the expense of the rest of the family. A key part of balance is making sure that the child with a disability fits within the family rather than overshadowing the family.

If one continues to try to fix the child, to overdo, to aspire for perfection instead of appreciating the child's qualities, the family is ripe for disappointment. Of course, it's natural to feel dejected at times. But if a family strives to achieve balanced needs, it becomes more resilient and emotionally healthy.

Healthy families—including the child with the disability—take turns. Family members help each other by supporting each other, and the child with the disability contributes to the family welfare as best he or she can. It's important to meet the challenges and needs of that child, but it's equally important to prioritize yourself and your other children as well.

Each family has its own timetable and its own journey, which can't be compared to other families. In fact, I've discouraged parents from comparing themselves to other families who appear to be coping more effectively than they. Your experiences are unique.

We're all fortunate to live now when society is now beginning to understand that a disability is secondary to the person, and that the person with a disability should be recognized as a person first, with feelings and reactions like everyone else. With changes in laws and inclusion in schools and after-school programs, the disabled are now part of the mainstream, and adults must accept that their children might be bringing home playmates with disabilities.

Many excellent resources exist for parents. Taking advantage of parent support groups, sensitive therapists, and a raft of commendable after-school programs will definitely lighten the load, but parents must reach out, ask for help, and find out what has worked for other parents. Doing so will make you aware that you aren't alone.

# Epilogue

"In this life we cannot do great things.
We can only do small things with great love."

—*Mother Teresa*

It's been a very long time since those early days of misery and angst. It took years before I realized that Dana was exactly who she was supposed to be. She was put on this earth for a greater good. And, indeed, she accomplished it.

If someone would've told me back then that giving birth to a child with disabilities would forever change me in a positive way, I never would've believed it. I was so hard on myself, feeling so ill equipped and unforgiving. But Dana changed me in ways that I couldn't then imagine. It was through her that I chose the work I do. It was through Dana that I healed myself. It was through her that I learned to lend a helping hand to parents by letting them know they're not alone, supporting them as they adjust to their crisis. And it was through her that KIT came to be created and many children were positively transformed.

Of all the challenges life presents us, nothing is more important than our roles as parents—yet that's the very task for which we're least prepared. Every family, I found, has to learn to adapt to new experiences in ways that are best for them and for their children. Each child is unique and cannot be raised by one set of given rules, especially if the child has a disability. While the children are developing, so, too, are the parents learning. They're in uncharted territory, feeling their way as their children grow.

Again, here's the key: Parents must understand and appreciate their children's attributes instead of only focusing on their struggles. Having realistic expectations comes from seeing the real child, not the child you want to see. The chronically disappointed parent has to get over it. Yes, times are tougher for the child with the disability. But the small successes feel even greater when the parents notice them. I've seen time and again how developing that kind of appreciation made a huge difference for parents. As a result, their children brought joy and love into their families in ways they never expected.

Sharing my journey with you, the reader, has allowed me to reflect on my life. I pray that my story will make a difference to you, perhaps allowing you to find your own special meaning. When I began writing this book, the aim wasn't just to share my story about having a child with a severe disability. I also wanted to describe my process of growth—through pain, loss and grieving—to a surprisingly joyous outcome. I hope you come away with a new understanding that there's no wrong or right paths, only *human* ways to live through difficult times.

In writing this story, I was surprised to learn how, after 53 years, the memories still caused me to well up and bring tears. When writing about my daughter Dana, I realized that my experiences with her will always remain a very tender and important part of me. Times have changed since Dana was born. Special education then was extremely limited and virtually non-existent after the age of three. Nothing existed for her and for children like her. Now there is help and hope in the growing network for children with disabilities and their families.

All along the way, I've been fortunate to meet people who've unwittingly helped me make good choices. From the young doctor at UCLA, who fired me from my volunteer position as counselor to the parents there and set me on my career path... to the executive director of the Jewish Community Foundation, who just happened to be visiting our home and coincidentally mentioned a bequest that had been left to serve children with disabilities...to Mary Shea, the first person I met in San Diego, who was working on a grant to include children with disabilities in preschools.

Though unanticipated, these people didn't pass by without notice. If I've learned anything, it's to pay attention to coincidences, to pay attention to the messages that are sent our way. Often, we're so busy focusing on what needs to get done that we don't notice the wonderful people who are walking by. Luckily, I was able to seize those moments to pursue my dreams, and I've never regretted that for a moment.

I've met some people who attempt to deal with uncertainty by planning to experience joy "later," who believe that the speed and complexity of what's happening looms so large there's no room now for joy and happiness. Thus, they wait for the perfect time and space, as if that exists.

But I'd suggest that happiness must be seized whenever chances appear. Celebrate birthdays, first occasions and those private special moments. Find and foster love whenever you can. Be slow to anger and quick to forgive. Make compassion a major focus of your life.

As the poet William Blake wrote, "He who grabs the joys as they fly lives on eternity's sunrise." So seize those small moments, practice those small kindnesses so that you never look back on your life and realize you didn't allow yourself to live and savor the joy of your journey.

# Acknowledgments

*W*riting this book included an interesting twist in that my first editor, Jacquie Ibrahim, was someone sent to interview me about KIT. After having heard my story, she urged me to write this book. I explained to Jacquie that I'd already tried authoring a book years before but put it aside when I went to work developing KIT. After much cajoling from Jacquie and with her persistent offers to assist me, I agreed to write the book. The result was a true collaborative labor of love, working with and becoming close to Jacquie. She encouraged and spurred me on to write every step of the way. When I was struggling with concepts, she had the ability to explain clearly what I was trying to express, and her eloquent words and phrases captured the essence of the important elements of my life experiences.

I'm also grateful to Dale Fetherling, my second editor, who patiently helped me construct this puzzle into an orderly memoir. He understood everything I was trying to express and was able to cut and paste this labor of love with eloquent ease.

Jacquie, Dale, the parents, the children and many others have been gifts given to me to help me help others. They've all been among my private, special people. My relationships with the parents with whom I have come in contact over the years have fortified me and strengthened my resolve to continue to help them. If my work has made a difference for parents in helping them find balance between hope and despair, between realism and denial, between appreciation and desperation, then I have found the real meaning of fulfillment, knowing that Dana's life was meant to be.

Printed in the United States
131505LV00004B/4/P

9 781600 375378